OLD MOO

Horoscope and Astral Diary

AQUARIUS

OLD MOORE'S

HOROSCOPE AND ASTRAL DIARY

AQUARIUS

foulsham
LONDON • NEW YORK • TORONTO • SYDNEY

W. Foulsham & Co. Ltd
for Foulsham Publishing Ltd
The Old Barrel Store, Drayman's Lane, Marlow, Bucks SL7 2FF

Foulsham books can be found in all good bookshops and direct from
www.foulsham.com

ISBN: 978-0-572-04735-1

Copyright © 2018 Foulsham Publishing Ltd

A CIP record for this book is available from the British Library

All rights reserved

The Copyright Act prohibits (subject to certain very limited
exceptions) the making of copies of any copyright work or
of a substantial part of such a work, including the making
of copies by photocopying or similar process. Written
permission to make a copy or copies must therefore
normally be obtained from the publisher in advance. It is
advisable also to consult the publisher if in any doubt as to
the legality of any copying which is to be undertaken.

Printed in Great Britain by Martins The Printers, Berwick-upon-Tweed

CONTENTS

1	Introduction	6
2	The Essence of Aquarius: Exploring the Personality of Aquarius the Water Carrier	7
3	Aquarius on the Cusp	13
4	Aquarius and its Ascendants	16
5	The Moon and the Part it Plays in your Life	24
6	Moon Signs	28
7	Aquarius in Love	32
8	Venus: The Planet of Love	36
9	Venus through the Zodiac Signs	38
10	The Astral Diary: How the Diagrams Work	42
11	Aquarius: Your Year in Brief	44
12	Aquarius 2019: Diary Pages	45
13	How to Calculate Your Rising Sign	124
14	Rising Signs for Aquarius	125
15	The Zodiac, Planets and Correspondences	127

INTRODUCTION

Astrology has been a part of life for centuries now, and no matter how technological our lives become, it seems that it never diminishes in popularity. For thousands of years people have been gazing up at the star-clad heavens and seeing their own activities and proclivities reflected in the movement of those little points of light. Across centuries countless hours have been spent studying the way our natures, activities and decisions seem to be paralleled by their predictable movements. Old Moore, a time-served veteran in astrological research, continues to monitor the zodiac and has produced the Astral Diary for 2019, tailor-made to your own astrological makeup.

Old Moore's Astral Diary is unique in its ability to get the heart of your nature and to offer you the sort of advice that might come from a trusted friend. It enables you to see in a day-by-day sense exactly how the planets are working for you. The diary section advises how you can get the best from upcoming situations and allows you to plan ahead successfully. There's also room on each daily entry to record your own observations or appointments.

While other popular astrology books merely deal with your astrological 'Sun sign', the Astral Diaries go much further. Every person on the planet is unique and Old Moore allows you to access your individuality in a number of ways. The front section gives you the chance to work out the placement of the Moon at the time of your birth and to see how its position has set an important seal on your overall nature. Perhaps most important of all, you can use the Astral Diary to discover your Rising Sign. This is the zodiac sign that was appearing over the Eastern horizon at the time of your birth and is just as important to you as an individual as is your Sun sign.

It is the synthesis of many different astrological possibilities that makes you what you are and with the Astral Diaries you can learn so much. How do you react to love and romance? Through the unique Venus tables and the readings that follow them, you can learn where the planet Venus was at the time of your birth. It is even possible to register when little Mercury is 'retrograde', which means that it appears to be moving backwards in space when viewed from the Earth. Mercury rules communication, so be prepared to deal with a few setbacks in this area when you see the sign ☿. The Astral Diary will be an interest and a support throughout the whole year ahead.

Old Moore extends his customary greeting to all people of the Earth and offers his age-old wishes for a happy and prosperous period ahead.

THE ESSENCE OF AQUARIUS

Exploring the Personality of Aquarius the Water Carrier

(21ST JANUARY – 19TH FEBRUARY)

What's in a sign?

Oh, what a wonderful person you can be! Despite a number of contradictions and one of the most complicated natures to be found anywhere in the zodiac, you certainly know how to make friends and influence people. Your ruling planet is Uranus, one of the more recently discovered members of the solar system's family. It rules modern communications, such as radio and television, and also has a response to the recent discoveries of science. It is within the world of 'the modern' that you reside and you have little or no difficulty keeping up with the ever-increasing pace of life.

People naturally like you and it's not surprising. You are open, liberal, and rarely judgmental, and you are often surrounded by deeply original and even eccentric types. Life to you is a storybook full of fascinating tales. Aquarians amass information 'on the hoof' and very little passes you by. Understanding what makes others tick is meat and drink to you and proves to be a source of endless joy. Unlike the other Air signs of Gemini and Libra, you are able to spend long hours on your own if necessary and always keep your mind active.

Aquarians have great creative potential; they are refined, often extremely well educated and they remain totally classless. This makes it easy for you to get on with just about any sort of person and also explains your general success in the material world. You are fascinating, original, thought-provoking and even quite deep on occasions. Matters that take months for others to synthesise, you can absorb in minutes. It is clear to everyone that you are one of life's natural leaders, but when you head any organisation you do so by co-operation and example because you are not in the least authoritarian.

In love you can be ardent and sincere – for a while at least. You need to be loved and it's true that deeply personal relationships can be a problem to you if they are not supplying what is most important to you. Few people know the real you, because your nature exists on so many different levels. For this reason alone you defy analysis and tend to remain outside the scope of orthodoxy. And because people can't weigh you up adequately, you appear to be more fascinating than ever.

Aquarius resources

Your chief resource has to be originality. Like a precious Fabergé Egg you are a single creation, unique and quite unlike anything else to be found anywhere in the world. Of course, used wrongly, this can make you seem odd or even downright peculiar. But Aquarians usually have a knack for creating the best possible impression. The chances are that you dress in your own way and speak the words that occur to you, and that you have a side to your nature that shuns convention. Despite this you know how to adapt when necessary. As a result your dinner parties would sport guests of a wide variety of types and stations. All of these people think they know the 'real you' and remain committed to helping you as much as they can.

The natural adaptability that goes along with being an Aquarian makes it possible for you to turn your hand to many different projects. And because you are from an Air sign, you can undertake a variety of tasks at the same time. This makes for a busy life, but being on the go is vital for you and you only tire when you are forced into jobs that you find demeaning, pointless or downright dull.

All of the above combines to make a nature that has 'resourcefulness' as its middle name. Arriving at a given set of circumstances – say a specific task that has to be undertaken – you first analyse what is required. Having done so you get cracking and invariably manage to impress all manner of people with your dexterity, attention to detail and downright intelligence. You can turn work into a social event, or derive financial gain from your social life. Activity is the keyword and you don't really differentiate between the various components of life as many people would.

Success depends on a number of different factors. You need to be doing things you enjoy as much you can and you simply cannot be held back or bound to follow rules that appear to make no sense to you. You respond well to kindness, and generally receive it because you are so considerate yourself. But perhaps your greatest skill of all is your ability to make a silk purse out of a sow's ear. You are never stuck for an idea and rarely let financial restrictions get in your way.

Beneath the surface

'What you see is what you get' could never really be considered a sensible or accurate statement when applied to the sign of Aquarius. It's difficult enough for you to know the way your complicated mind works, and almost impossible for others to sort out the tangle of possibilities. Your mind can be as untidy as a tatty workbox on occasions and yet at other times you can see through situations with a clarity that would dazzle almost any observer. It really depends on a whole host of circumstances, some of which are inevitably beyond your own control. You are at your best when you are allowed to take charge from the very start of any project, because then your originality of thought comes into play. Your sort of logic is unique to you, so don't expect anyone else to go down the same mental routes that you find easy to follow.

Aquarians are naturally kind and don't tend to discriminate. This is not a considered matter, it's simply the way you are. As a result it is very hard for you to understand prejudice, or individuals who show any form of intolerance. The fairness that you exemplify isn't something that you have to work at – it comes as naturally to you as breathing does.

You can be very peculiar and even a little cranky on occasions. These aspects of your nature are unlikely to have any bearing on your overall popularity, but they do betray a rather unusual mindset that isn't like that of any other zodiac sign. When you feel stressed you tend to withdraw into yourself, which is not really good for you. A much better strategy would be to verbalise what you are thinking, even though this is not always particularly easy to do.

There are many people in the world who think they know you well, but each and every one of them knows only one Aquarian. There are always more, each a unique individual and probably as much of a mystery to you as they would be to all your relatives and friends, that is if any of them suspected just how deep and mysterious you can be. Despite these facts, your mind is clear and concise, enabling you to get to the truth of any given situation almost immediately. You should never doubt your intuitive foresight and, in the main, must always back your hunches. It is rare indeed for you to be totally wrong about the outcome of any potential situation and your genuine originality of thought is the greatest gift providence has bestowed on you.

Making the best of yourself

Interacting with the world is most important to you. Although you can sometimes be a good deal quieter than the other Air signs of Gemini and Libra, you are still a born communicator, with a great need to live your life to the full. If you feel hemmed in or constrained by circumstances, you are not going to show your best face to family, friends or colleagues. That's why you must move heaven and earth to make certain that you are not tied down in any way. Maintaining a sense of freedom is really just a mental state to Aquarius but it is absolutely vital to your well-being.

As far as work is concerned you need to be doing something that allows you the room you need to move. Any occupation that means thinking on your feet would probably suit you fine. All the same you feel more comfortable in administrative surroundings, rather than getting your hands dirty. Any profession that brings change and variety on a daily basis would be best. You are a good team operator, and yet can easily lead from the front. Don't be frightened to show colleagues that you have an original way of looking at life and that you are an inveterate problem solver.

In terms of friendship you tend to be quite catholic in your choice of pals. Making the best of yourself means keeping things that way. You are not naturally jealous yourself but you do tend to attract friends who are. Make it plain that you can't tie yourself down to any one association, no matter how old or close it may be. At least if you do this nobody can suggest that they weren't warned when you wander off to talk to someone else. Personal relationships are a different matter, though it's hardly likely that you would live in the pocket of your partner. In any situation you need space to breathe, and this includes romantic attachments. People who know you well will not try to hem you in.

Don't be frightened to show your unconventional, even wild side to the world at large. You are a bold character, with a great deal to say and a natural warmth that could melt an iceberg. This is the way providence made you and it is only right to use your gifts to the full.

The impressions you give

You are not a naturally secretive person and don't hold back very much when it comes to speaking your mind. It might be suggested therefore that the external and internal Aquarian is more or less the same person. Although generally true, it has to be remembered that you have a multi-faceted nature and one that adapts quickly to changing circumstances. It is this very adaptability that sets you apart in the eyes of the world.

You often make decisions based on intuitive foresight and although many Aquarians are of above average intelligence, you won't always make use of a deep knowledge of any given situation. In essence you often do what seems right, though you tend to act whilst others are still standing around and thinking. This makes you good to have around in a crisis and convinces many of those looking on that you are incredibly capable, relaxed and confident. Of course this isn't always the case, but even a nervous interior tends to breed outward action in the case of your zodiac sign, so the world can be forgiven for jumping to the wrong conclusion.

People like you – there's no doubt about that. However, you must realise that you have a very upfront attitude, which on occasions is going to get you into trouble. Your occasional weirdness, rather than being a turn-off, is likely to stimulate the interest that the world has in you. Those with whom you come into contact invariably find your personality to be attractive, generous, high-spirited and refreshing. For all these reasons it is very unlikely that you would actually make many enemies, even if some folk are clearly jealous of the easy way you have with the world.

One of the great things about Aquarians is that they love to join in. As a result you may find yourself doing all sorts of things that others would find either difficult or frightening. You can be zany, wild and even mad on occasions, but these tendencies will only get you liked all the more. The world will only tire of you if you allow yourself to get down in the dumps or grumpy – a very rare state for Aquarius.

The way forward

In terms of living your life to the full it is probable that you don't need any real advice from an astrologer. Your confidence allows you to go places that would make some people shiver, whilst your intuitive foresight gives you the armoury you need to deal with a world that can sometimes seem threatening. Yet for all this you are not immune to mental turmoil on occasions, and probably spend rather too much time in the fast lane. It's good to rest, a fact that you need to remember the next time you find yourself surrounded by twenty-seven jobs, all of which you are trying to undertake at the same time.

The more the world turns in the direction of information technology, the happier you are likely to become. If others have difficulty in this age of computers, it's likely that you relish the challenges and the opportunities that these artificial intelligences offer. You are happy with New Age concepts and tend to look at the world with compassion and understanding. Despite the fact that you are always on the go, it's rare for you to be moving forward so fast that you forget either the planet that brought you to birth, or the many underprivileged people who inhabit parts of it. You have a highly developed conscience and tend to work for the good of humanity whenever you can.

You might not be constructed of the highest moral fibre known to humanity, a fact that sometimes shows when it comes to romantic attachments. Many Aquarians play the field at some time in their lives and it's certain that you need a personal relationship that keeps you mentally stimulated. Although your exterior can sometimes seem superficial, you have a deep and sensitive soul – so perhaps you should marry a poet, or at least someone who can cope with the twists and turns of the Aquarian mind. Aquarians who tie themselves down too early, or to the wrong sort of individual, invariable end up regretting the fact.

You can be deeply creative and need to live in clean and cheerful surroundings. Though not exactly a minimalist you don't like clutter and constantly need to spring-clean your home – and your mind. Living with others isn't difficult for you, in fact it's essential. Since you are so adaptable you fit in easily to almost any environment, though you will always ultimately stamp your own character onto it. You love to be loved and offer a great deal in return, even if you are occasionally absent when people need you the most. In essence you are in love with life and so perhaps you should not be too surprised to discover that it is very fond of you too.

AQUARIUS ON THE CUSP

Old Moore is often asked how astrological profiles are altered for those people born at either the beginning or the end of a zodiac sign, or, more properly, on the cusps of a sign. In the case of Aquarius this would be on the 21st of January and for two or three days after, and similarly at the end of the sign, probably from the 17th to the 19th of February. In this year's Astral Diaries, once again, Old Moore sets out to explain the differences regarding cuspid signs.

The Capricorn Cusp – January 21st to 23rd

What really sets you apart is a genuinely practical streak that isn't always present in the sign of Aquarius when taken alone. You are likely to have all the joy of life and much of the devil-may-care attitude of your Sun sign, but at the same time you are capable of getting things done in a very positive way. This makes you likely to achieve a higher degree of material success and means that you ally managerial skills with the potential for rolling up your sleeves and taking part in the 'real work' yourself. Alongside this you are able to harness the naturally intuitive qualities of Aquarius in a very matter-of-fact way. Few people would have the ability to pull the wool over your eyes and you are rarely stuck for a solution, even to apparently difficult problems.

You express yourself less well than Aquarius taken alone, and you may have a sort of reserve that leads others to believe that your mind is full of still waters which run very deep. The air of mystery can actually be quite useful, because it masks an ability to react and move quickly when necessary, which is a great surprise to the people around you. However, there are two sides to every coin and if there is a slightly negative quality to this cuspid position it might lie in the fact that you are not quite the communicator that tends to be the case with Aquarius, and you could go through some fairly quiet and introspective phases that those around you would find somewhat difficult to understand. In a positive sense this offers a fairly wistful aspect to your nature that may, in romantic applications, appear very attractive. There is something deeply magnetic about your nature and it isn't quite possible for everyone to understand what makes you tick. Actually this is part of your appeal because there is nothing like curiosity on the part of others to enhance your profile.

Getting things done is what matters the most to you, harnessed to the ability to see the wider picture in life. It's true that not everyone understands your complex nature, but in friendship you are scarcely short of supportive types. Family members can be especially important to you and personal attachments are invariably made for life.

The Pisces Cusp – February 17th to 19th

It appears that you are more of a thinker than most and achieve depths of contemplation that would be totally alien to some signs of the zodiac. Much of your life is given over to the service you show for humanity as a whole but you don't sink into the depths of despair in the way that some Piscean individuals are inclined to do. You are immensely likeable and rarely stuck for a good idea. You know how to enjoy yourself, even if this quality is usually tied to the support and assistance that you constantly give to those around you.

Many of you will already have chosen a profession that somehow fulfils your need to be of service, and it isn't unusual for Pisces-cusp Aquarians to alter their path in life totally if it isn't fulfilling this most basic requirement. When necessary, you can turn your hand to almost anything, generally giving yourself totally to the task in hand, sometimes to the exclusion of everything else. People with this combination often have two very different sorts of career, sometimes managing to do both at the same time. Confidence in practical matters isn't usually lacking, even if you sometimes think that your thought processes are a little bit muddled.

In love you are ardent and more sincere than Aquarius sometimes seems to be. There can be a tinge of jealousy at work now and again in deep relationships, but you are less likely than Pisces to let this show. You tend to be very protective of the people who are most important in your life and these are probably fewer in number than often seems to be the case for Aquarius. Your love of humanity and the needs it has of you are of supreme importance and you barely let a day pass without offering some sort of assistance. For this reason, and many others, you are a much loved individual and show your most caring face to the world for the majority of your life. Material success can be hard to come by at first, but it isn't really an aspect of life that worries you too much in any case. It is far more important for you to be content with your lot and, if you are happy, it seems that more or less everything else tends to follow.

AQUARIUS AND ITS ASCENDANTS

The nature of every individual on the planet is composed of the rich variety of zodiac signs and planetary positions that were present at the time of their birth. Your Sun sign, which in your case is Aquarius, is one of the many factors when it comes to assessing the unique person you are. Probably the most important consideration, other than your Sun sign, is to establish the zodiac sign that was rising over the eastern horizon at the time that you were born. This is your Ascending or Rising sign. Most popular astrology fails to take account of the Ascendant, and yet its importance remains with you from the very moment of your birth, through every day of your life. The Ascendant is evident in the way you approach the world, and so, when meeting a person for the first time, it is this astrological influence that you are most likely to notice first. Our Ascending sign essentially represents what we appear to be, while the Sun sign is what we feel inside ourselves.

The Ascendant also has the potential for modifying our overall nature. For example, if you were born at a time of day when Aquarius was passing over the eastern horizon (this would be around the time of dawn) then you would be classed as a double Aquarian. As such, you would typify this zodiac sign, both internally and in your dealings with others. However, if your Ascendant sign turned out to be a Fire sign, such as Aries, there would be a profound alteration of nature, away from the expected qualities of Aquarius.

One of the reasons why popular astrology often ignores the Ascendant is that it has always been rather difficult to establish. Old Moore has found a way to make this possible by devising an easy-to-use table, which you will find on page 125 of this book. Using this, you can establish your Ascendant sign at a glance. You will need to know your rough time of birth, then it is simply a case of following the instructions.

For those readers who have no idea of their time of birth it might be worth allowing a good friend, or perhaps your partner, to read through the section that follows this introduction. Someone who deals with you on a regular basis may easily discover your Ascending sign, even though you could have some difficulty establishing it for yourself. A good understanding of this component of your nature is essential if you want to be aware of that 'other person' who is responsible for the way you make contact with the world at large. Your Sun sign, Ascendant sign, and the other pointers in this book will, together, allow you a far better understanding of what makes you tick as an individual. Peeling back the different layers of your astrological make-up can be an enlightening experience, and the Ascendant may represent one of the most important layers of all.

Aquarius with Aquarius Ascendant

You are totally unique and quite original, so much so that very few people could claim to understand what makes you tick. Routines get on your nerves and you need to be out there doing something most of the time. Getting where you want to go in life isn't too difficult, except that when you arrive, your destination might not look half so interesting as it did before. You are well liked and should have many friends. This is not to say that your pals have much in common with each other, because you choose from a wide cross-section of people. Although folks see you as being very reasonable in the main, you are capable of being quite cranky on occasions. Your intuition is extremely strong and is far less likely to let you down than would be the case with some individuals.

Travel is very important to you and you will probably live for some time in a different part of your own country, or even in another part of the world. At work you are more than capable, but do need something to do that you find personally stimulating, because you are not very good at constant routine. You can be relied upon to use your originality and find solutions that are instinctive and brilliant. Most people are very fond of you.

Aquarius with Pisces Ascendant

Here we find the originality of Aquarius balanced by the very sensitive qualities of Pisces, and it makes for a very interesting combination. When it comes to understanding other people you are second to none, but it's certain that you are more instinctive than either Pisces or Aquarius when taken alone. You are better at routines than Aquarius, but also relish a challenge more than the typical Piscean would. Active and enterprising, you tend to know what you want from life, but consideration of others, and the world at large, will always be part of the scenario. People with this combination often work on behalf of humanity and are to be found in social work, the medical profession and religious institutions. As far as beliefs are concerned you don't conform to established patterns, and yet may get closer to the truth of the Creator than many deep theological thinkers have ever been able to do. Acting on impulse as much as you do means that not everyone understands the way your mind works, but your popularity will invariably see you through.

Passionate and deeply sensitive, you are able to negotiate the twists and turns of a romantic life that is hardly likely to be run-of-the-mill. In the end, however, you should be able to discover a very deep personal and spiritual happiness.

Aquarius with Aries Ascendant

If ever anyone could be accused of setting off immediately, but slowly, it has to be you. These are very contradictory signs and the differences will express themselves in a variety of ways. One thing is certain, you have tremendous tenacity and will see a job through patiently from beginning to end, without tiring on the way and ensuring that every detail is taken care of properly. This combination often brings good health and a great capacity for continuity, particularly in terms of the length of life. You are certainly not as argumentative as the typical Aries, but you do know how to get your own way, which is just as well because you are usually thinking on behalf of everyone else and not just on your own account.

At home you can relax, which is a blessing for Aries, though in fact you seldom choose to do so because you always have some project or other on the go. You probably enjoy knocking down and rebuilding walls, though this is a practical tendency and not responsive to relationships, in which you are ardent and sincere. Impetuosity is as close to your heart as is the case for any type of subject, though you certainly have the ability to appear patient and steady. But it's just a front, isn't it?

Aquarius with Taurus Ascendant

There is nothing that you fail to think about deeply and with great intensity. You are wise, honest and very scientific in your approach to life. Routines are necessary in life but you have most of them sorted out well in advance and so always have time to look at the next interesting fact. If you don't spend all your time watching documentaries on the television set, you make a good friend and love to socialise. Most of the great discoveries of the world were probably made by people with this sort of astrological combination, though your nature is rather 'odd' on occasions and so can be rather difficult for others to understand.

You may be most surprised when others tell you that you are eccentric, but you don't really mind too much because for half of the time you are not inhabiting the same world as the rest of us. Because you can be delightfully dotty you are probably much loved and cherished by your friends, of which there are likely to be many. Family members probably adore you too, and you can be guaranteed to entertain anyone with whom you come into contact. The only fly in the ointment is that you sometimes lose track of reality, whatever that might be, and fly high in your own atmosphere of rarefied possibilities.

Aquarius with Gemini Ascendant

If you were around in the 1960s there is every chance that you were the first to go around with flowers in your hair. You are unconventional, original, quirky and entertaining. Few people would fail to notice your presence and you take life as it comes, even though on most occasions you are firmly in the driving seat. It all probability you care very much about the planet on which you live and the people with whom you share it. Not everyone understands you, but that does not really matter, for you have more than enough communication skills to put your message across intact. You should avoid wearing yourself out by worrying about things that you cannot control, and you definitely gain from taking time out to meditate. However, whether or not you allow yourself that luxury remains to be seen.

If you are not the most communicative form of Gemini subject then you must come a close second. Despite this fact much of what you have to say makes real sense and you revel in the company of interesting, intelligent and stimulating people, whose opinions on a host of matters will add to your own considerations. You are a true original in every sense of the word and the mere fact of your presence in the world is bound to add to the enjoyment of life experienced by the many people with whom you make contact.

Aquarius with Cancer Ascendant

The truly original spark, for which the sign of Aquarius is famed, can only enhance the caring qualities of Cancer, and is also inclined to bring the Crab out of its shell to a much greater extent than would be the case with certain other zodiac combinations. Aquarius is a party animal and never arrives without something interesting to say, which is doubly the case when the reservoir of emotion and consideration that is Cancer is feeding the tap. Your nature can be rather confusing for even you to deal with, but you are inspirational, bright, charming and definitely fun to be around.

The Cancer element in your nature means that you care about your home and the people to whom you are related. You are also a good and loyal friend, who would keep attachments for much longer than could be expected for Aquarius alone. You love to travel and can be expected to make many journeys to far-off places during your life. Some attention will have to be paid to your health, because you are capable of burning up masses of nervous energy, often without getting the periods of rest and contemplation that are essential to the deeper qualities of the sign of Cancer. Nevertheless you have determination, resilience and a refreshing attitude that lifts the spirits of the people in your vicinity.

Aquarius with Leo Ascendant

All associations with Aquarius bring originality, and you are no exception. You aspire to do your best most of the time but manage to achieve your objectives in an infinitely amusing and entertaining way. Not that you set out to do so, because if you are an actor on the stage of life, it seems as though you are a natural one. There is nothing remotely pretentious about your breezy personality or your ability to occupy the centre of any stage. This analogy is quite appropriate because you probably like the theatre. Being in any situation when reality is suspended for a while suits you down to the ground, and in any case you may regularly ask yourself if you even recognise what reality is. Always asking questions, both of yourself and the world at large, you soldier on relentlessly, though not to the exclusion of having a good time on the way.

Keeping to tried and tested paths is not your way. You are a natural trailblazer who is full of good ideas and who has the energy to put them into practice. You care deeply for the people who play an important part in your life but are wise enough to allow them the space they need to develop their own personalities along the way. Most people like you, many love you, and one or two think that you really are the best thing since sliced bread.

Aquarius with Virgo Ascendant

How could anyone make the convention unconventional? Well, if anyone can manage, you can. There are great contradictions here, because on the one hand you always want to do the expected thing, but the Aquarian quality within your nature loves to surprise everyone on the way. If you don't always know what you are thinking or doing, it's a pretty safe bet that others won't either, so it's important on occasions really to stop and think. However this is not a pressing concern, because you tend to live a fairly happy life and muddle through no matter what. Other people tend to take to you well and it is likely that you will have many friends. You tend to be bright and cheerful and can approach even difficult tasks with the certainty that you have the skills necessary to see them through to their conclusion. Give and take are important factors in the life of any individual and particularly so in your case. Because you can stretch yourself in order to understand what makes other people think and act in the way that they do, you have the reputation of being a good friend and a reliable colleague.

In love you can be somewhat more fickle than the typical Virgoan, and yet you are always interesting to live with. Where you are, things happen, and you mix a sparkling wit with deep insights.

Aquarius with Libra Ascendant

Stand by for a truly interesting and very inspiring combination here, but one that is sometimes rather difficult to fathom, even for the sort of people who believe themselves to be very perceptive. The reason for this could be that any situation has to be essentially fixed and constant in order to get a handle on it, and this is certainly not the case for the Aquarian–Libran type. The fact is that both these signs are Air signs, and to a certain extent as unpredictable as the wind itself.

To most people you seem to be original, frank, free and very outspoken. Not everything you do makes sense to others and if you were alive during the hippy era, it is likely that you went around with flowers in your hair, for you are a free-thinking idealist at heart. With age you mature somewhat, but never too much, because you will always see the strange, the comical and the original in life. This is what keeps you young and is one of the factors that makes you so very attractive to members of the opposite sex. Many people will want to 'adopt' you and you are at your very best when in company.

Much of your effort is expounded on others and yet, unless you discipline yourself a good deal, personal relationships of the romantic sort can bring certain difficulties. Careful planning is necessary.

Aquarius with Scorpio Ascendant

Here we have a combination that shows much promise and a flexibility that allows many changes in direction, allied to a power to succeed, sometimes very much against all the odds. Aquarius lightens the load of the Scorpio mind, turning the depths into potential, and intuitive foresight into a means for getting on in life. There are depths here, because even airy Aquarius isn't so easy to understand, and it is therefore a fact that some people with this combination will always be something of a mystery. However, even this fact can be turned to your advantage because it means that people will always be looking at you. Confidence is so often the key to success in life and the Scorpio–Aquarius mix offers this, or at least appears to do so. Even when this is not entirely the case, the fact that everyone around you believes it to be true is often enough.

You are usually good to know, and show a keen intellect and a deep intelligence, aided by a fascination for life that knows no bounds. When at your best you are giving, understanding, balanced and active. On those occasions when things are not going well for you, beware of a stubborn streak and the need to be sensational. Keep it light and happy and you won't go far wrong. Most of you are very, very much loved.

Aquarius with Sagittarius Ascendant

There is an original streak to your nature which is very attractive to the people with whom you share your life. Always different, ever on the go and anxious to try out the next experiment in life, you are interested in almost everything, and yet deeply attached to almost nothing. Everyone you know thinks that you are a little 'odd', but you probably don't mind them believing this because you know it to be true. In fact it is possible that you positively relish your eccentricity, which sets you apart from the common herd and means that you are always going to be noticed.

Although it may seem strange with this combination of Air and Fire, you can be distinctly cool on occasions, have a deep and abiding love of your own company now and again and won't be easily understood. Love comes fairly easily to you but there are times when you are accused of being self-possessed, self-indulgent and not willing enough to fall in line with the wishes of those around you. Despite this you walk on and on down your own path. At heart you are an extrovert and you love to party, often late into the night. Luxury appeals to you, though it tends to be of the transient sort. Travel could easily play a major and a very important part in your life.

Aquarius with Capricorn Ascendant

Here the determination of Capricorn is assisted by a slightly more adaptable quality and an off-beat personality that tends to keep everyone else guessing. You don't care to be quite so predictable as the archetypal Capricorn would be, and there is a more idealistic quality here, or at least one that shows more. A greater number of friends than Capricorn usually keeps is likely, though less than the true Aquarian would gather. Few people doubt your sincerity, though by no means all of them understand what makes you tick. Unfortunately you are not in a position to help them out, because you are not too sure yourself. All the same, you muddle through and can be very capable when the mood takes you.

Being a natural traveller, you love to see new places and would be quite fascinated by cultures that are very different to your own. People with this combination are inclined to spend some time living abroad and may even settle there. You look out for the underdog and will always have time for a good cause, no matter what it takes to help. In romantic terms you are a reliable partner, though with a slightly wayward edge which, if anything, tends to make you even more attractive. Listen to your intuition, which is well honed and rarely lets you down. Generally speaking you are very popular.

THE MOON AND THE PART IT PLAYS IN YOUR LIFE

In astrology the Moon is probably the single most important heavenly body after the Sun. Its unique position, as partner to the Earth on its journey around the solar system, means that the Moon appears to pass through the signs of the zodiac extremely quickly. The zodiac position of the Moon at the time of your birth plays a great part in personal character and is especially significant in the build-up of your emotional nature.

Sun Moon Cycles

The first lunar cycle deals with the part the position of the Moon plays relative to your Sun sign. I have made the fluctuations of this pattern easy for you to understand by means of a simple cyclic graph. It appears on the first page of each 'Your Month At A Glance', under the title 'Highs and Lows'. The graph displays the lunar cycle and you will soon learn to understand how its movements have a bearing on your level of energy and your abilities.

Your Own Moon Sign

Discovering the position of the Moon at the time of your birth has always been notoriously difficult because tracking the complex zodiac positions of the Moon is not easy. This process has been reduced to three simple stages with Old Moore's unique Lunar Tables. A breakdown of the Moon's zodiac positions can be found from page 28 onwards, so that once you know what your Moon Sign is, you can see what part this plays in the overall build-up of your personal character.

If you follow the instructions on the next page you will soon be able to work out exactly what zodiac sign the Moon occupied on the day that you were born and you can then go on to compare the reading for this position with those of your Sun sign and your Ascendant. It is partly the comparison between these three important positions that goes towards making you the unique individual you are.

HOW TO DISCOVER YOUR MOON SIGN

This is a three-stage process. You may need a pen and a piece of paper but if you follow the instructions below the process should only take a minute or so.

STAGE 1 First of all you need to know the Moon Age at the time of your birth. If you look at Moon Table 1, on page 26, you will find all the years between 1920 and 2018 down the left side. Find the year of your birth and then trace across to the right to the month of your birth. Where the two intersect you will find a number. This is the date of the New Moon in the month that you were born. You now need to count forward the number of days between the New Moon and your own birthday. For example, if the New Moon in the month of your birth was shown as being the 6th and you were born on the 20th, your Moon Age Day would be 14. If the New Moon in the month of your birth came after your birthday, you need to count forward from the New Moon in the previous month. If you were born in a Leap Year, remember to count the 29th February. You can tell if your birth year was a Leap Year if the last two digits can be divided by four. Whatever the result, jot this number down so that you do not forget it.

STAGE 2 Take a look at Moon Table 2 on page 27. Down the left hand column look for the date of your birth. Now trace across to the month of your birth. Where the two meet you will find a letter. Copy this letter down alongside your Moon Age Day.

STAGE 3 Moon Table 3 on page 27 will supply you with the zodiac sign the Moon occupied on the day of your birth. Look for your Moon Age Day down the left hand column and then for the letter you found in Stage 2. Where the two converge you will find a zodiac sign and this is the sign occupied by the Moon on the day that you were born.

Your Zodiac Moon Sign Explained

You will find a profile of all zodiac Moon Signs on pages 28 to 31, showing in yet another way how astrology helps to make you into the individual that you are. In each daily entry of the Astral Diary you can find the zodiac position of the Moon for every day of the year. This also allows you to discover your lunar birthdays. Since the Moon passes through all the signs of the zodiac in about a month, you can expect something like twelve lunar birthdays each year. At these times you are likely to be emotionally steady and able to make the sort of decisions that have real, lasting value.

Moon Table 1

YEAR	DEC	JAN	FEB	YEAR	DEC	JAN	FEB	YEAR	DEC	JAN	FEB
1921	29	9	8	1954	25	5	3	1987	20	29	28
1922	18	27	26	1955	14	24	22	1988	9	19	17
1923	8	17	15	1956	2	13	11	1989	28	7	6
1924	26	6	5	1957	21	1/30	–	1990	17	26	25
1925	15	24	23	1958	10	19	18	1991	6	15	14
1926	5	14	12	1959	29	9	7	1992	24	4	3
1927	24	3	2	1960	18	27	26	1993	14	23	22
1928	12	21	19	1961	7	16	15	1994	2	11	10
1929	1/30	11	9	1962	26	6	5	1995	22	1/30	–
1930	19	29	28	1963	15	25	23	1996	10	20	18
1931	9	18	17	1964	4	14	13	1997	28	9	7
1932	27	7	6	1965	22	3	1	1998	18	27	26
1933	17	25	24	1966	12	21	19	1999	7	17	16
1934	6	15	14	1967	1/30	10	9	2000	26	6	4
1935	25	5	3	1968	20	29	28	2001	15	25	23
1936	13	24	22	1969	9	19	17	2002	4	13	12
1937	2	12	11	1970	28	7	6	2003	23	3	1
1938	21	1/31	–	1971	17	26	25	2004	11	21	20
1939	10	20	19	1972	6	15	14	2005	30	10	9
1940	28	9	8	1973	25	5	4	2006	20	29	28
1941	18	27	26	1974	14	24	22	2007	9	18	16
1942	8	16	15	1975	3	12	11	2008	27	8	6
1943	27	6	4	1976	21	1/31	29	2009	16	26	25
1944	15	25	24	1977	10	19	18	2010	6	15	14
1945	4	14	12	1978	29	9	7	2011	25	4	3
1946	23	3	2	1979	18	27	26	2012	12	23	22
1947	12	21	19	1980	7	16	15	2013	2	12	10
1948	1/30	11	9	1981	26	6	4	2014	2	1/31	–
1949	19	29	27	1982	15	25	23	2015	20	19	20
1950	9	18	16	1983	4	14	13	2016	29	9	8
1951	28	7	6	1984	22	3	1	2017	18	27	25
1952	17	26	25	1985	12	21	19	2018	07	16	15
1953	6	15	14	1986	1/30	10	9	2019	26	05	04

Table 2

DAY	JAN	FEB
1	A	D
2	A	D
3	A	D
4	A	D
5	A	D
6	A	D
7	A	D
8	A	D
9	A	D
10	A	E
11	B	E
12	B	E
13	B	E
14	B	E
15	B	E
16	B	E
17	B	E
18	B	E
19	B	E
20	B	F
21	C	F
22	C	F
23	C	F
24	C	F
25	C	F
26	C	F
27	C	F
28	C	F
29	C	F
30	C	–
31	D	–

Table 3

M/D	A	B	C	D	E	F	G
0	CP	AQ	AQ	AQ	PI	PI	PI
1	AQ	AQ	AQ	PI	PI	PI	AR
2	AQ	AQ	PI	PI	PI	AR	AR
3	AQ	PI	PI	PI	AR	AR	AR
4	PI	PI	AR	AR	AR	AR	TA
5	PI	AR	AR	AR	TA	TA	TA
6	AR	AR	AR	TA	TA	TA	GE
7	AR	AR	TA	TA	TA	GE	GE
8	AR	TA	TA	TA	GE	GE	GE
9	TA	TA	GE	GE	GE	CA	CA
10	TA	GE	GE	GE	CA	CA	CA
11	GE	GE	GE	CA	CA	CA	LE
12	GE	GE	CA	CA	CA	LE	LE
13	GE	CA	CA	LE	LE	LE	LE
14	CA	CA	LE	LE	LE	VI	VI
15	CA	LE	LE	LE	VI	VI	VI
16	LE	LE	LE	VI	VI	VI	LI
17	LE	LE	VI	VI	VI	LI	LI
18	LE	VI	VI	VI	LI	LI	LI
19	VI	VI	VI	LI	LI	LI	SC
20	VI	LI	LI	LI	SC	SC	SC
21	LI	LI	LI	SC	SC	SC	SA
22	LI	LI	SC	SC	SC	SA	SA
23	LI	SC	SC	SC	SA	SA	SA
24	SC	SC	SC	SA	SA	SA	CP
25	SC	SA	SA	SA	CP	CP	CP
26	SA	SA	SA	CP	CP	CP	AQ
27	SA	SA	CP	CP	AQ	AQ	AQ
28	SA	CP	CP	AQ	AQ	AQ	AQ
29	CP	CP	CP	AQ	AQ	AQ	PI

AR = Aries, TA = Taurus, GE = Gemini, CA = Cancer, LE = Leo, VI = Virgo, LI = Libra, SC = Scorpio, SA = Sagittarius, CP = Capricorn, AQ = Aquarius, PI = Pisces

MOON SIGNS

Moon in Aries

You have a strong imagination, courage, determination and a desire to do things in your own way and forge your own path through life.

Originality is a key attribute; you are seldom stuck for ideas although your mind is changeable and you could take the time to focus on individual tasks. Often quick-tempered, you take orders from few people and live life at a fast pace. Avoid health problems by taking regular time out for rest and relaxation.

Emotionally, it is important that you talk to those you are closest to and work out your true feelings. Once you discover that people are there to help, there is less necessity for you to do everything yourself.

Moon in Taurus

The Moon in Taurus gives you a courteous and friendly manner, which means you are likely to have many friends.

The good things in life mean a lot to you, as Taurus is an Earth sign that delights in experiences which please the senses. Hence you are probably a lover of good food and drink, which may in turn mean you need to keep an eye on the bathroom scales, especially as looking good is also important to you.

Emotionally you are fairly stable and you stick by your own standards. Taureans do not respond well to change. Intuition also plays an important part in your life.

Moon in Gemini

You have a warm-hearted character, sympathetic and eager to help others. At times reserved, you can also be articulate and chatty: this is part of the paradox of Gemini, which always brings duplicity to the nature. You are interested in current affairs, have a good intellect, and are good company and likely to have many friends. Most of your friends have a high opinion of you and would be ready to defend you should the need arise. However, this is usually unnecessary, as you are quite capable of defending yourself in any verbal confrontation.

Travel is important to your inquisitive mind and you find intellectual stimulus in mixing with people from different cultures. You also gain much from reading, writing and the arts but you do need plenty of rest and relaxation in order to avoid fatigue.

Moon in Cancer

The Moon in Cancer at the time of birth is a fortunate position as Cancer is the Moon's natural home. This means that the qualities of compassion and understanding given by the Moon are especially enhanced in your nature, and you are friendly and sociable and cope well with emotional pressures. You cherish home and family life, and happily do the domestic tasks. Your surroundings are important to you and you hate squalor and filth. You are likely to have a love of music and poetry.

Your basic character, although at times changeable like the Moon itself, depends on symmetry. You aim to make your surroundings comfortable and harmonious, for yourself and those close to you.

Moon in Leo

The best qualities of the Moon and Leo come together to make you warmhearted, fair, ambitious and self-confident. With good organisational abilities, you invariably rise to a position of responsibility in your chosen career. This is fortunate as you don't enjoy being an 'also-ran' and would rather be an important part of a small organisation than a menial in a large one.

You should be lucky in love, and happy, provided you put in the effort to make a comfortable home for yourself and those close to you. It is likely that you will have a love of pleasure, sport, music and literature. Life brings you many rewards, most of them as a direct result of your own efforts, although you may be luckier than average and ready to make the best of any situation.

Moon in Virgo

You are endowed with good mental abilities and a keen receptive memory, but you are never ostentatious or pretentious. Naturally quite reserved, you still have many friends, especially of the opposite sex. Marital relationships must be discussed carefully and worked at so that they remain harmonious, as personal attachments can be a problem if you do not give them your full attention.

Talented and persevering, you possess artistic qualities and are a good homemaker. Earning your honours through genuine merit, you work long and hard towards your objectives but show little pride in your achievements. Many short journeys will be undertaken in your life.

Moon in Libra

With the Moon in Libra you are naturally popular and make friends easily. People like you, probably more than you realise, you bring fun to a party and are a natural diplomat. For all its good points, Libra is not the most stable of astrological signs and, as a result, your emotions can be a little unstable too. Therefore, although the Moon in Libra is said to be good for love and marriage, your Sun sign and Rising sign will have an important effect on your emotional and loving qualities.

You must remember to relate to others in your decision-making. Co-operation is crucial because Libra represents the 'balance' of life that can only be achieved through harmonious relationships. Conformity is not easy for you because Libra, an Air sign, likes its independence.

Moon in Scorpio

Some people might call you pushy. In fact, all you really want to do is to live life to the full and protect yourself and your family from the pressures of life. Take care to avoid giving the impression of being sarcastic or impulsive and use your energies wisely and constructively.

You have great courage and you invariably achieve your goals by force of personality and sheer effort. You are fond of mystery and are good at predicting the outcome of situations and events. Travel experiences can be beneficial to you.

You may experience problems if you do not take time to examine your motives in a relationship, and also if you allow jealousy, always a feature of Scorpio, to cloud your judgement.

Moon in Sagittarius

The Moon in Sagittarius helps to make you a generous individual with humanitarian qualities and a kind heart. Restlessness may be intrinsic as your mind is seldom still. Perhaps because of this, you have a need for change that could lead you to several major moves during your adult life. You are not afraid to stand your ground when you know your judgement is right, you speak directly and have good intuition.

At work you are quick, efficient and versatile and so you make an ideal employee. You need work to be intellectually demanding and do not enjoy tedious routines.

In relationships, you anger quickly if faced with stupidity or deception, though you are just as quick to forgive and forget. Emotionally, there are times when your heart rules your head.

Moon in Capricorn

The Moon in Capricorn makes you popular and likely to come into the public eye in some way. The watery Moon is not entirely comfortable in the Earth sign of Capricorn and this may lead to some difficulties in the early years of life. An initial lack of creative ability and indecision must be overcome before the true qualities of patience and perseverance inherent in Capricorn can show through.

You have good administrative ability and are a capable worker, and if you are careful you can accumulate wealth. But you must be cautious and take professional advice in partnerships, as you are open to deception. You may be interested in social or welfare work, which suit your organisational skills and sympathy for others.

Moon in Aquarius

The Moon in Aquarius makes you an active and agreeable person with a friendly, easy-going nature. Sympathetic to the needs of others, you flourish in a laid-back atmosphere. You are broad-minded, fair and open to suggestion, although sometimes you have an unconventional quality which others can find hard to understand.

You are interested in the strange and curious, and in old articles and places. You enjoy trips to these places and gain much from them. Political, scientific and educational work interests you and you might choose a career in science or technology.

Money-wise, you make gains through innovation and concentration and Lunar Aquarians often tackle more than one job at a time. In love you are kind and honest.

Moon in Pisces

You have a kind, sympathetic nature, somewhat retiring at times, but you always take account of others' feelings and help when you can.

Personal relationships may be problematic, but as life goes on you can learn from your experiences and develop a better understanding of yourself and the world around you.

You have a fondness for travel, appreciate beauty and harmony and hate disorder and strife. You may be fond of literature and would make a good writer or speaker yourself. You have a creative imagination and may come across as an incurable romantic. You have strong intuition, maybe bordering on a mediumistic quality, which sets you apart from the mass. You may not be rich in cash terms, but your personal gifts are worth more than gold.

AQUARIUS IN LOVE

Discover how compatible in love you are with people from the same and other signs of the zodiac. Five stars equals a match made in heaven!

Aquarius meets Aquarius

This is a good match for several reasons. Most importantly, although it sounds arrogant, Aquarians like themselves. At its best, Aquarius is one of the fairest, most caring and genuinely pleasant zodiac signs and so it is only when faced by the difficulties created by others that it shows a less favourable side. Put two Aquarians together and voilà – instant success! Personal and family life should bring more joy. On the whole, a platform for adventure based on solid foundations. Star rating: *****

Aquarius meets Pisces

Zodiac signs that follow each other often have something in common, but this is not the case with Aquarius and Pisces. Both signs are deeply caring, but in different ways. Pisces is one of the deepest zodiac signs, and Aquarius simply isn't prepared to embark on the journey. Pisceans, meanwhile, would probably find Aquarians superficial and even flippant. On the positive side there is potential for a well-balanced relationship, but unless one party is untypical of their zodiac sign, it often doesn't get started. Star rating: **

Aquarius meets Aries

Aquarius is an Air sign, and Air and Fire often work well together, but not in the case of Aries and Aquarius. The average Aquarian lives in what the Ram sees as a fantasy world, so a meeting of minds is unlikely. Of course, the dominant side of Aries could be trained by the devil-may-care attitude of Aquarius. There are meeting points but they are difficult to establish. However, given sufficient time and an open mind on both sides, a degree of happiness is possible. Star rating: **

Aquarius meets Taurus

In any relationship of which Aquarius is a part, surprises abound. It is difficult for Taurus to understand the soul-searching, adventurous, changeable Aquarian, but on the positive side, the Bull is adaptable and can respond well to a dose of excitement. Aquarians are kind and react well to the same quality coming back at them. Both are friendly, capable of deep affection and basically creative. Unfortunately, Taurus simply doesn't know what makes Aquarius tick, which could lead to feelings of isolation, even if these don't always show on the surface. Star rating: **

Aquarius meets Gemini

Aquarius is commonly mistaken for a Water sign, but in fact it's ruled by the Air element, and this is the key to its compatibility with Gemini. Both signs mix freely socially, and each has an insatiable curiosity. There is plenty of action, lots of love, but very little rest, and so great potential for success if they don't wear each other out! Aquarius revels in its own eccentricity, and encourages Gemini to emulate this. Theirs will be an unconventional household, but almost everyone warms to this crazy and unpredictable couple. Star rating: *****

Aquarius meets Cancer

Cancer is often attracted to Aquarius and, as Aquarius is automatically on the side of anyone who fancies it, so there is the potential for something good here. Cancer loves Aquarius' devil-may-care approach to life, but also recognises and seeks to strengthen the basic lack of self-confidence that all Air signs try so hard to keep secret. Both signs are natural travellers and are quite adventurous. Their family life could be unusual, but friends would recognise a caring, sharing household with many different interests shared by people genuinely in love. Star rating: ***

Aquarius meets Leo

The problem here is that Aquarius doesn't think in the general sense of the word, it knows. Leo, on the other hand, is more practical and relies more on logical reasoning, and consequently it doesn't understand Aquarius very well. Aquarians can also appear slightly frosty in their appreciation of others and this, too, will annoy Leo. This is a good match for a business partnership because Aquarius is astute, while Leo is brave, but personally the prognosis is less promising. Tolerance, understanding and forbearance are all needed to make this work. Star rating: **

Aquarius meets Virgo

Aquarius is a strange sign because no matter how well one knows it, it always manages to surprise. For this reason, against the odds, it's quite likely that Aquarius will form a sucessful relationship with Virgo. Aquarius is changeable, unpredictable and often quite odd, while Virgo is steady, a fuss-pot and very practical. Herein lies the key. What one sign needs, the other provides and that may be the surest recipe for success imaginable. On-lookers may not know why the couple are happy, but they will recognise that this is the case. Star rating: ****

Aquarius meets Libra

One of the best combinations imaginable, partly because both are Air signs and so share a common meeting point. But perhaps the more crucial factor is that both signs respect each other. Aquarius loves life and originality, and is quite intellectual. Libra is similar, but more balanced and rather less eccentric. A visit to this couple's house would be entertaining and full of zany wit, activity and excitement. Both are keen to travel and may prefer to 'find themselves' before taking on too many domestic responsibilities. Star rating: *****

Aquarius meets Scorpio

This is a promising and practical combination. Scorpio responds well to Aquarius' persistent exploration of its deep nature and so this generally shy sign becomes lighter, brighter and more inspirational. Meanwhile, Aquarians are rarely as sure of themselves as they like to appear and are reassured by Scorpio's constant, steady and determined support. Both signs want to be kind to each other, which is a good starting point to a relationship that should be warm most of the time and extremely hot occasionally. Star rating: ****

Aquarius meets Sagittarius

Both Sagittarius and Aquarius are into mind games, which may lead to something of an intellectual competition. If one side is happy to be 'bamboozled' it won't be a problem, but it is more likely that the relationship will turn into a competition, which won't auger well for its long-term future. However, on the plus side, both signs are adventurous and sociable, so as long as there is always something new and interesting to do, the match could turn out very well. Star rating: **

Aquarius meets Capricorn

Probably one of the least likely combinations, as Capricorn and Aquarius are unlikely to choose each other in the first place, unless one side is quite untypical of their sign. Capricorn approaches things in a practical way and likes to get things done, while Aquarius works almost exclusively for the moment and relies heavily on intuition. Their attitudes to romance are also diametrically opposed: Aquarius' moods tend to swing from red hot to ice cold in a minute, which is alien to steady Capricorn. Star rating: **

VENUS:
THE PLANET OF LOVE

If you look up at the sky around sunset or sunrise you will often see Venus in close attendance to the Sun. It is arguably one of the most beautiful sights of all and there is little wonder that historically it became associated with the goddess of love. But although Venus does play an important part in the way you view love and in the way others see you romantically, this is only one of the spheres of influence that it enjoys in your overall character.

Venus has a part to play in the more cultured side of your life and has much to do with your appreciation of art, literature, music and general creativity. Even the way you look is responsive to the part of the zodiac that Venus occupied at the start of your life, though this fact is also down to your Sun sign and Ascending sign. If, at the time you were born, Venus occupied one of the more gregarious zodiac signs, you will be more likely to wear your heart on your sleeve, as well as to be more attracted to entertainment, social gatherings and good company. If on the other hand Venus occupied a quiet zodiac sign at the time of your birth, you would tend to be more retiring and less willing to shine in public situations.

It's good to know what part the planet Venus plays in your life, for it can have a great bearing on the way you appear to the rest of the world and since we all have to mix with others, you can learn to make the very best of what Venus has to offer you.

One of the great complications in the past has always been trying to establish exactly what zodiac position Venus enjoyed when you were born, because the planet is notoriously difficult to track. However, I have solved that problem by creating a table that is exclusive to your Sun sign, which you will find on the following page.

Establishing your Venus sign could not be easier. Just look up the year of your birth on the page opposite and you will see a sign of the zodiac. This was the sign that Venus occupied in the period covered by your sign in that year. If Venus occupied more than one sign during the period, this is indicated by the date on which the sign changed, and the name of the new sign. For instance, if you were born in 1945, Venus was in Pisces until the 12th February, after which time it was in Aries. If you were born before 12th February your Venus sign is Pisces, if you were born on or after 12th February, your Venus sign is Aries. Once you have established the position of Venus at the time of your birth, you can then look in the pages which follow to see how this has a bearing on your life as a whole.

Venus: The Planet of Love

1921 PISCES / 15.2 ARIES
1922 CAPRICORN / 25.1 AQUARIUS / 18.2 PISCES
1923 SAGITTARIUS / 7.2 CAPRICORN
1924 PISCES / 13.2 ARIES
1925 CAPRICORN / 9.2 AQUARIUS
1926 AQUARIUS
1927 AQUARIUS / 2.2 PISCES
1928 SAGITTARIUS / 29.1 CAPRICORN
1929 PISCES / 14.2 ARIES
1930 CAPRICORN / 25.1 AQUARIUS / 18.2 PISCES
1931 SAGITTARIUS / 6.2 CAPRICORN
1932 PISCES / 13.2 ARIES
1933 CAPRICORN / 8.2 AQUARIUS
1934 AQUARIUS
1935 AQUARIUS / 2.2 PISCES
1936 SAGITTARIUS / 29.1 CAPRICORN
1937 PISCES / 13.2 ARIES
1938 CAPRICORN / 24.1 AQUARIUS / 17.2 PISCES
1939 SAGITTARIUS / 6.2 CAPRICORN
1940 PISCES / 12.2 ARIES
1941 CAPRICORN / 8.2 AQUARIUS
1942 AQUARIUS
1943 AQUARIUS / 1.2 PISCES
1944 SAGITTARIUS / 28.1 CAPRICORN
1945 PISCES / 12.2 ARIES
1946 CAPRICORN / 24.1 AQUARIUS / 17.2 PISCES
1947 SAGITTARIUS / 6.2 CAPRICORN
1948 PISCES / 12.2 ARIES
1949 CAPRICORN / 7.2 AQUARIUS
1950 AQUARIUS
1951 AQUARIUS / 1.2 PISCES
1952 SAGITTARIUS / 27.1 CAPRICORN
1953 PISCES / 11.2 ARIES
1954 CAPRICORN / 23.1 AQUARIUS / 16.2 PISCES
1955 SAGITTARIUS / 6.2 CAPRICORN
1956 PISCES / 11.2 ARIES
1957 CAPRICORN / 7.2 AQUARIUS
1958 AQUARIUS
1959 AQUARIUS / 31.1 PISCES
1960 SAGITTARIUS / 27.1 CAPRICORN
1961 PISCES / 9.2 ARIES
1962 CAPRICORN / 23.1 AQUARIUS / 15.2 PISCES
1963 SAGITTARIUS / 6.2 CAPRICORN
1964 PISCES / 11.2 ARIES
1965 CAPRICORN / 6.2 AQUARIUS
1966 AQUARIUS
1967 AQUARIUS / 30.1 PISCES
1968 SAGITTARIUS / 26.1 CAPRICORN
1969 PISCES / 7.2 ARIES
1970 CAPRICORN / 22.1 AQUARIUS / 15.2 PISCES

1971 SAGITTARIUS / 5.2 CAPRICORN
1972 PISCES / 10.2 ARIES
1973 CAPRICORN / 5.2 AQUARIUS
1974 AQUARIUS / 7.2 CAPRICORN
1975 AQUARIUS / 30.1 PISCES
1976 SAGITTARIUS / 26.1 CAPRICORN
1977 PISCES / 5.2 ARIES
1978 CAPRICORN / 22.1 AQUARIUS / 14.2 PISCES
1979 SAGITTARIUS / 5.2 CAPRICORN
1980 PISCES / 10.2 ARIES
1981 CAPRICORN / 5.2 AQUARIUS
1982 AQUARIUS / 29.1 CAPRICORN
1983 AQUARIUS / 29.1 PISCES
1984 SAGITTARIUS / 25.1 CAPRICORN
1985 PISCES / 5.2 ARIES
1986 AQUARIUS / 14.2 PISCES
1987 SAGITTARIUS / 5.2 CAPRICORN
1988 PISCES / 9.2 ARIES
1989 CAPRICORN / 4.2 AQUARIUS
1990 AQUARIUS / 23.1 CAPRICORN
1991 AQUARIUS / 29.1 PISCES
1992 SAGITTARIUS / 25.1 CAPRICORN
1993 PISCES / 4.2 ARIES
1994 AQUARIUS / 13.2 PISCES
1995 SAGITTARIUS / 5.2 CAPRICORN
1996 PISCES / 9.2 ARIES
1997 CAPRICORN / 4.2 AQUARIUS
1998 AQUARIUS / 23.1 CAPRICORN
1999 AQUARIUS / 29.1 PISCES
2000 SAGITTARIUS / 25.1 CAPRICORN
2001 PISCES / 4.2 ARIES
2002 AQUARIUS / 13.2 PISCES
2003 SAGITTARIUS
2004 PISCES / 9.2 AQUARIUS
2005 CAPRICORN / 6.2 AQUARIUS
2006 AQUARIUS / 14.1 CAPRICORN
2007 AQUARIUS / 29.1 PISCES
2008 SAGITTARIUS / 25.1 CAPRICORN
2009 PISCES / 4.2 ARIES
2010 AQUARIUS / 12.2 PISCES
2011 SAGITTARIUS
2012 PISCES / 9.2 AQUARIUS
2013 CAPRICORN / 6.2 AQUARIUS
2014 CAPRICORN / 6.2 AQUARIUS
2015 AQUARIUS / 29.1 PISCES
2016 SAGITTARIUS / 24.1 AQUARIUS
2017 PISCES / 4.2 ARIES
2018 AQUARIUS / 12.2 PISCES
2019 SAGITTARIUS

VENUS THROUGH THE ZODIAC SIGNS

Venus in Aries

Amongst other things, the position of Venus in Aries indicates a fondness for travel, music and all creative pursuits. Your nature tends to be affectionate and you would try not to create confusion or difficulty for others if it could be avoided. Many people with this planetary position have a great love of the theatre, and mental stimulation is of the greatest importance. Early romantic attachments are common with Venus in Aries, so it is very important to establish a genuine sense of romantic continuity. Early marriage is not recommended, especially if it is based on sympathy. You may give your heart a little too readily on occasions.

Venus in Taurus

You are capable of very deep feelings and your emotions tend to last for a very long time. This makes you a trusting partner and lover, whose constancy is second to none. In life you are precise and careful and always try to do things the right way. Although this means an ordered life, which you are comfortable with, it can also lead you to be rather too fussy for your own good. Despite your pleasant nature, you are very fixed in your opinions and quite able to speak your mind. Others are attracted to you and historical astrologers always quoted this position of Venus as being very fortunate in terms of marriage. However, if you find yourself involved in a failed relationship, it could take you a long time to trust again.

Venus in Gemini

As with all associations related to Gemini, you tend to be quite versatile, anxious for change and intelligent in your dealings with the world at large. You may gain money from more than one source but you are equally good at spending it. There is an inference here that you are a good communicator, via either the written or the spoken word, and you love to be in the company of interesting people. Always on the look-out for culture, you may also be very fond of music, and love to indulge the curious and cultured side of your nature. In romance you tend to have more than one relationship and could find yourself associated with someone who has previously been a friend or even a distant relative.

Venus in Cancer

You often stay close to home because you are very fond of family and enjoy many of your most treasured moments when you are with those you love. Being naturally sympathetic, you will always do anything you can to support those around you, even people you hardly know at all. This charitable side of your nature is your most noticeable trait and is one of the reasons why others are naturally so fond of you. Being receptive and in some cases even psychic, you can see through to the soul of most of those with whom you come into contact. You may not commence too many romantic attachments but when you do give your heart, it tends to be unconditionally.

Venus in Leo

It must become quickly obvious to almost anyone you meet that you are kind, sympathetic and yet determined enough to stand up for anyone or anything that is truly important to you. Bright and sunny, you warm the world with your natural enthusiasm and would rarely do anything to hurt those around you, or at least not intentionally. In romance you are ardent and sincere, though some may find your style just a little overpowering. Gains come through your contacts with other people and this could be especially true with regard to romance, for love and money often come hand in hand for those who were born with Venus in Leo. People claim to understand you, though you are more complex than you seem.

Venus in Virgo

Your nature could well be fairly quiet no matter what your Sun sign might be, though this fact often manifests itself as an inner peace and would not prevent you from being basically sociable. Some delays and even the odd disappointment in love cannot be ruled out with this planetary position, though it's a fact that you will usually find the happiness you look for in the end. Catapulting yourself into romantic entanglements that you know to be rather ill-advised is not sensible, and it would be better to wait before you committed yourself exclusively to any one person. It is the essence of your nature to serve the world at large and through doing so it is possible that you will attract money at some stage in your life.

Venus in Libra

Venus is very comfortable in Libra and bestows upon those people who have this planetary position a particular sort of kindness that is easy to recognise. This is a very good position for all sorts of friendships and also for romantic attachments that usually bring much joy into your life. Few individuals with Venus in Libra would avoid marriage and since you are capable of great depths of love, it is likely that you will find a contented personal life. You like to mix with people of integrity and intelligence but don't take kindly to scruffy surroundings or work that means getting your hands too dirty. Careful speculation, good business dealings and money through marriage all seem fairly likely.

Venus in Scorpio

You are quite open and tend to spend money quite freely, even on those occasions when you don't have very much. Although your intentions are always good, there are times when you get yourself in to the odd scrape and this can be particularly true when it comes to romance, which you may come to late or from a rather unexpected direction. Certainly you have the power to be happy and to make others contented on the way, but you find the odd stumbling block on your journey through life and it could seem that you have to work harder than those around you. As a result of this, you gain a much deeper understanding of the true value of personal happiness than many people ever do, and are likely to achieve true contentment in the end.

Venus in Sagittarius

You are lighthearted, cheerful and always able to see the funny side of any situation. These facts enhance your popularity, which is especially high with members of the opposite sex. You should never have to look too far to find romantic interest in your life, though it is just possible that you might be too willing to commit yourself before you are certain that the person in question is right for you. Part of the problem here extends to other areas of life too. The fact is that you like variety in everything and so can tire of situations that fail to offer it. All the same, if you choose wisely and learn to understand your restless side, then great happiness can be yours.

Venus in Capricorn

The most notable trait that comes from Venus in this position is that it makes you trustworthy and able to take on all sorts of responsibilities in life. People are instinctively fond of you and love you all the more because you are always ready to help those who are in any form of need. Social and business popularity can be yours and there is a magnetic quality to your nature that is particularly attractive in a romantic sense. Anyone who wants a partner for a lover, a spouse and a good friend too would almost certainly look in your direction. Constancy is the hallmark of your nature and unfaithfulness would go right against the grain. You might sometimes be a little too trusting.

Venus in Aquarius

This location of Venus offers a fondness for travel and a desire to try out something new at every possible opportunity. You are extremely easy to get along with and tend to have many friends from varied backgrounds, classes and inclinations. You like to live a distinct sort of life and gain a great deal from moving about, both in a career sense and with regard to your home. It is not out of the question that you could form a romantic attachment to someone who comes from far away or be attracted to a person of a distinctly artistic and original nature. What you cannot stand is jealousy, for you have friends of both sexes and would want to keep things that way.

Venus in Pisces

The first thing people tend to notice about you is your wonderful, warm smile. Being very charitable by nature you will do anything to help others, even if you don't know them well. Much of your life may be spent sorting out situations for other people, but it is very important to feel that you are living for yourself too. In the main, you remain cheerful, and tend to be quite attractive to members of the opposite sex. Where romantic attachments are concerned, you could be drawn to people who are significantly older or younger than yourself or to someone with a unique career or point of view. It might be best for you to avoid marrying whilst you are still very young.

HOW THE DIAGRAMS WORK

Through the picture diagrams in the Astral Diary I want to help you to plot your year. With them you can see where the positive and negative aspects will be found in each month. To make the most of them, all you have to do is remember where and when!

Let me show you how they work ...

THE MONTH AT A GLANCE

Just as there are twelve separate zodiac signs, so astrologers believe that each sign has twelve separate aspects to life. Each of the twelve segments relates to a different personal aspect. I list them all every month so that their meanings are always clear.

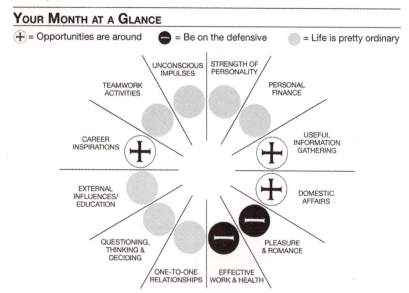

I have designed this chart to show you how and when these twelve different aspects are being influenced throughout the year. When there is a shaded circle, nothing out of the ordinary is to be expected. However, when a circle turns white with a plus sign, the influence is positive. Where the circle is black with a minus sign, it is a negative.

YOUR ENERGY RHYTHM CHART

Below is a picture diagram in which I link your zodiac group to the rhythm of the Moon. In doing this I have calculated when you will be gaining strength from its influence and equally when you may be weakened by it.

If you think of yourself as being like the tides of the ocean then you may understand how your own energies must also rise and fall. And if you understand how it works and when it is working, then you can better organise your activities to achieve more and get things done more easily.

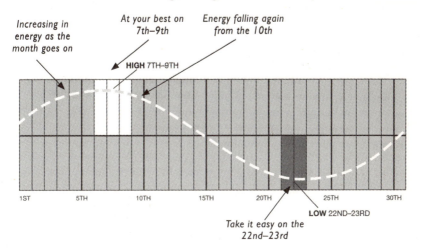

THE KEY DAYS

Some of the entries are in **bold**, which indicates the working of astrological cycles in your life. Look out for them each week as they are the best days to take action or make decisions. The daily text tells you which area of your life to focus on.

MERCURY RETROGRADE

The Mercury symbol (☿) indicates that Mercury is retrograde on that day. Since Mercury governs communication, the fact that it appears to be moving backwards when viewed from the Earth at this time should warn you that your communication skills are not likely to be at their best and you could expect some setbacks.

AQUARIUS: YOUR YEAR IN BRIEF

The year gets off to an interesting start for Aquarius and allows you to utilise your very adaptable personality. Both January and February bring their own particular gains and the pace of life should increase as time passes. Not everyone will be following your lead in a professional sense but that probably won't bother you much because during this period you tend to lead by example. Friends should prove to be steadfast.

March and April can bring some Aquarians nearer to their heart's desire. Things are looking especially good in a romantic sense and as the world wakes up to a new spring, so your heart flutters in anticipation of romance. Money matters are likely to be variable but you know what you need to get by and won't be at all avaricious during this period. Some trends suggest you should take care what you are eating.

As the summer arrives, so May and June will find you looking for new things to do and for places to visit that you have not seen before. The better weather should entice you out of doors because that is where you will feel your greatest joy at this time, in the company of fun people. You might enjoy a little lucky streak and a little cautious speculation might seem more attractive than usual.

Along with the summer weather, July and August are likely to bring a great deal of heat into your life, too. This is the time when you sizzle romantically. Aquarians who have been looking for love should concentrate their efforts during the summer holiday season especially as it is likely you will travel at some point. People from the past may come back into your life and could bring with them a few surprises. Don't be too quick to judge the actions of a friend in August.

As autumn arrives, you put in all the effort necessary to get things done in a practical sense. While you may not be over-sensitive during September and October, you certainly know how to succeed. Not everyone is going to be on your side during this period but in truth it probably won't matter to you all that much because you are more than happy to follow your own lead. Confidence is king.

Things pep up noticeably as the year end approaches. Despite any distractions, both November and December see you anxious to make progress at home and at work. Socially speaking you are at your best, making new friendships and consolidating old ones. It seems you are flavour of the month, especially around Christmas-time, a period during which you can allow yourself a little sentimentality. End the year on a high and don't restrict your dreams for the future.

January 2019

Your Month at a Glance

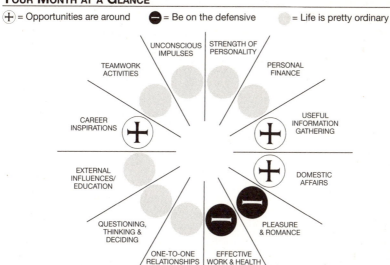

January Highs and Lows

Here I show you how the rhythms of the Moon will affect you this month. Like the tide, your energies and abilities will rise and fall with its pattern. When it is above the centre line, go for it, when it is below, you should be resting.

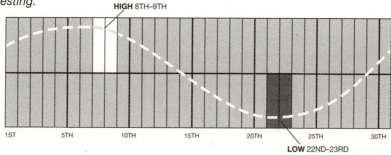

Your Daily Guide to January 2019

1 TUESDAY
Moon Age Day 25   Moon Sign Scorpio

The chart for Aquarius reveals that you are rather ahead of yourself as the new year begins, so you can afford to take stock of situations more than would generally be the case. You have some big plans in your mind, but it is going to take some time to get them off the ground. Today would be ideal for seeking support.

2 WEDNESDAY
Moon Age Day 26   Moon Sign Scorpio

Routines are definitely out of the window today, as you opt for a more exciting time. You need change and diversity, and that added zing you are feeling at present can be utilised in a number of different directions. Others may notice how good you are to have around and will not be afraid to make this known.

3 THURSDAY
Moon Age Day 27   Moon Sign Sagittarius

There are no real certainties today, only questions. You will be asking a fair number of them yourself, but that's fine with you because that is how you gather information. In sporting activities, you should go for gold, though silver or bronze is the most likely result right now. At work, you may be considering new responsibilities.

4 FRIDAY
Moon Age Day 28   Moon Sign Sagittarius

Someone you haven't seen for ages might be making a return visit to your life at any time now. In addition, you are likely to feel the need of a change of scene, which might involve travelling some distance. The fact that it's winter won't make any difference to you – you want to get moving.

5 SATURDAY
Moon Age Day 0   Moon Sign Capricorn

Creatively speaking, you are on top form today and might decide the time is right to make some changes in and around your home. If decorating is on the cards, you may well opt for bold colours, together with the very latest ideas in décor. Whether everyone in the family agrees with this remains to be seen.

6 SUNDAY
Moon Age Day 1   Moon Sign Capricorn

This Sunday should be a neutral day that leaves you free to occupy yourself in whatever manner you think best. If you want others on board, you might have to push them along. Try to stay away from everyday routines, some of which could prove extremely tedious right now.

Your Daily Guide to January 2019

7 MONDAY
Moon Age Day 2   Moon Sign Capricorn

People are just dying to get to know you now, and more than ever in a social sense. With excitement around every turn, it could be hard to concentrate on the matter at hand. Be aware, though, that trends suggest everything will not turn out the way you might expect, so you may need to curb your enthusiasm.

8 TUESDAY
Moon Age Day 3   Moon Sign Aquarius

It definitely is now your time of the month. The lunar high allows you to make use of that excellent personality, not only in a professional sense, but personally too. It wouldn't be fair to suggest that you will get everything your heart desires, but there are little triumphs in the offing.

9 WEDNESDAY
Moon Age Day 4   Moon Sign Aquarius

Keep up your efforts to get ahead, and don't be put off by the sort of people who love to bring others down. Irrespective of circumstance, you tend to go around today with a smile on your face. There are likely to be financial gains, brought about mainly as a result of some simple good luck.

10 THURSDAY
Moon Age Day 5   Moon Sign Pisces

Don't be too quick to volunteer today because others will take you at your word and you might end up far busier than you expected. Although you are your usual, cheery self, you may not feel quite as in tune with life today. Everyone needs a rest now and again and today could be your time.

11 FRIDAY
Moon Age Day 6   Moon Sign Pisces

There are some strategic gains to be made today, particularly in relationships. Although others could slightly misconstrue what you are trying to say, in the main you know how to get your message across succinctly and successfully. Your attitude today is balanced and very fair.

12 SATURDAY
Moon Age Day 7   Moon Sign Pisces

People who are important to you figure prominently in your thinking today. You now have more energy and a greater sense of determination to get ahead. Confronting issues that have a bearing on your family life could seem important but you need to speak to the people in question before you take any action.

Your Daily Guide to January 2019

13 SUNDAY
Moon Age Day 8   Moon Sign Aries

Routines can be something of a bind today. The truth is that you will want to be free to pursue whatever interests are uppermost in your mind at present and won't find it easy to concentrate on what seem like irrelevant details. Patience is required, and let's face it, you have more of that than most people.

14 MONDAY
Moon Age Day 9   Moon Sign Aries

Set your sights on a busy week, but one that can be very exciting too. What you need to do at present is to mix business and pleasure. If you manage to do so, you will make money for yourself and have a good time too. If you are not at work, a shopping trip could really appeal.

15 TUESDAY
Moon Age Day 10   Moon Sign Taurus

The past catches up with you in one way or another, even if it's just in the way you are thinking. Nostalgia is a natural part of today, but you must not allow it to rule the present or guide you for the future. Aquarians who are looking for a new job should keep their eyes open under the current trends.

16 WEDNESDAY
Moon Age Day 11   Moon Sign Taurus

Discuss all issues in order to enlist a little help. That way you will get plans off to an amazing start at a time when they stand a good chance of working out. Don't get caught up in any sort of red tape and if possible make sure that you can move in a certain direction before you begin to take steps.

17 THURSDAY
Moon Age Day 12   Moon Sign Taurus

A work situation is likely to put you in the picture and leads to further advancement of a sort you might not have been expecting. There are many surprises around at the moment and this justifies the confidence you have had for a while now. Your creative potential also seems especially good at the moment.

18 FRIDAY
Moon Age Day 13   Moon Sign Gemini

Your personal influence is strong and it's clear that you can make the best possible impression when it counts the most. Your confidence might be lacking early in the day but it won't be long before you realise you are flavour of the month, at least as far as a certain group of people are concerned. A good day for romance.

Your Daily Guide to January 2019

19 SATURDAY
Moon Age Day 14   Moon Sign Gemini

Travel at this time ought to provide the real emotional highlights of the day and there is a proper mix of business and pleasure possible around now. With everything to play for at work it looks as though those who have it in their power to make your life easier and more comfortable are noticing you.

20 SUNDAY
Moon Age Day 15   Moon Sign Cancer

Events taking place with friends or as part of a team are positively highlighted today, and are likely to come through your social life. Make today your own as much as you can and allow the slightly competitive side of your nature to shine through, even though you are definitely a team player at the moment.

21 MONDAY
Moon Age Day 16   Moon Sign Cancer

Someone could have been suggesting that you change your outlook and though you want to accommodate them if you can, Aquarius is rather more fixed in its attitudes at present than would usually be the case. You could try to at least give the impression that you are taking other people's opinions into account.

22 TUESDAY
Moon Age Day 17   Moon Sign Leo

The lunar low comes along and threatens to stop you in your tracks, as least in some respects. View today as an opportunity to take a rest. It's true that you won't get as much done as you might wish but there is nothing at all to prevent you from planning strategies for later so don't get worked up about it.

23 WEDNESDAY
Moon Age Day 18   Moon Sign Leo

Although you still won't be moving any mountains, stand by for some interesting and potentially lucrative news, which could arrive at any time now. You have been working very hard of late and it is possible that the rewards you have been seeking are not so far away.

24 THURSDAY
Moon Age Day 19   Moon Sign Virgo

Trends indicate that your mental focus is not all that it might be today. This might therefore not be the best time for major decision-making. Rather you should let others make some of the running whilst you take a back seat. In many ways you are clearing the decks for the sort of action you sense will be coming along soon.

Your Daily Guide to January 2019

25 FRIDAY
Moon Age Day 20 Moon Sign Virgo

Avoid acting on impulse at this time and wait until tomorrow, by which time trends change significantly and will allow you to move faster than they do at the moment. If you are thoughtful this merely means that you are laying out your plans in a sensible manner.

26 SATURDAY
Moon Age Day 21 Moon Sign Libra

Anything connected with leisure and romance is positively highlighted in your chart today. It might be good to simply please yourself today, on what is, after all, a Saturday. Any short outing or trip with friends is likely to be especially pleasurable and events today feed you with new ideas that lead to practical advancement in the future.

27 SUNDAY
Moon Age Day 22 Moon Sign Libra

Keep your eyes and ears open to discover what is going on in your immediate vicinity. Even listening to gossip can be rewarding at the moment and might lead you towards actions that will see you better off in some way. Some interesting characters could be entering your life at this time and bring interesting interludes.

28 MONDAY
Moon Age Day 23 Moon Sign Scorpio

Heavy responsibilities may be the order of the day and you can expect to feel them keenly at some stage. Watch how you deal with loved ones at present and be willing to listen to another point of view. You can make progress but it will be hard to influence situations as much as you might want to.

29 TUESDAY
Moon Age Day 24 Moon Sign Scorpio

Right now you will probably feel at your most active and attractive. The slight hiccup that came along yesterday is well out of the way and you won't be stuck for an answer, no matter how much you are put on the spot. There are gains to be made on the financial front because you are very sensible at the moment.

30 WEDNESDAY
Moon Age Day 25 Moon Sign Sagittarius

Fresh material plans may get underway today and if you have been thinking about making professional changes, this would be a good time to get on with them. You now have a good ability to influence others without having to try too hard. Routines can be dealt with in a flash, even if some of them annoy you.

Your Daily Guide to January 2019

31 THURSDAY
Moon Age Day 26   Moon Sign Sagittarius

This is a favourable period for your love life and a day during which you want to stay warm and comfortable with your partner or sweetheart. The very best side of Aquarius is now on display and it looks as though you can call in a few favours from people who would be only too willing to put themselves out on your behalf.

February 2019

Your Month at a Glance

⊕ = Opportunities are around   ⊖ = Be on the defensive   ○ = Life is pretty ordinary

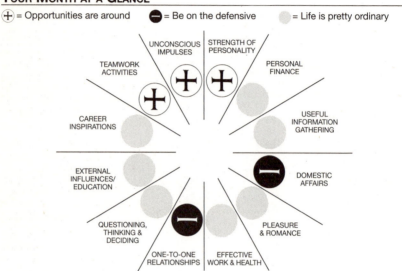

- UNCONSCIOUS IMPULSES ⊕
- STRENGTH OF PERSONALITY ⊕
- TEAMWORK ACTIVITIES ⊕
- PERSONAL FINANCE
- CAREER INSPIRATIONS
- USEFUL INFORMATION GATHERING
- EXTERNAL INFLUENCES/EDUCATION
- DOMESTIC AFFAIRS ⊖
- QUESTIONING, THINKING & DECIDING
- PLEASURE & ROMANCE
- ONE-TO-ONE RELATIONSHIPS ⊖
- EFFECTIVE WORK & HEALTH

February Highs and Lows

Here I show you how the rhythms of the Moon will affect you this month. Like the tide, your energies and abilities will rise and fall with its pattern. When it is above the centre line, go for it, when it is below, you should be resting.

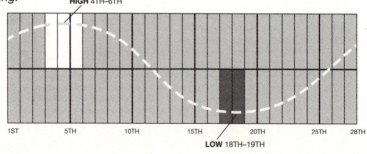

HIGH 4TH–6TH

LOW 18TH–19TH

52

Your Daily Guide to February 2019

1 FRIDAY *Moon Age Day 27   Moon Sign Sagittarius*

Although your ego is quite strong it is most likely that you will try to disguise this from others. This is a double-edged sword because you retain your modesty and yet fail to show the world at large how capable you are. In the end Aquarius can always find a sensible way forward and manage to please everyone.

2 SATURDAY *Moon Age Day 28   Moon Sign Capricorn*

This is a day when you will clearly avoid getting on the wrong side of others, especially family members. You are going to have to deal with a few very sensitive types right now and being careful comes as second nature to you. The attitude of friend may be better than that of family members right now.

3 SUNDAY *Moon Age Day 29   Moon Sign Capricorn*

This is a time when you can establish a very good dialogue with both colleagues and friends. Rules and regulations won't please you all that much and there is a strong chance that you want to find a new way forward at work. Your home life can be crowded by events but most of them are positive.

4 MONDAY *Moon Age Day 0   Moon Sign Aquarius*

The start of the week is particularly good, not least of all because the Moon is in your zodiac sign. It's fun and action from the word go, together with a real inclination to push back the boundaries of the possible. Getting family members to do your bidding should be really easy, in fact too easy for most Aquarians now.

5 TUESDAY *Moon Age Day 1   Moon Sign Aquarius*

Although you can expect some small setbacks today, these merely act as extra incentives to make you push to find new ground, and they therefore won't stand in your way at all. What you are looking for most of all is change and diversity, together with a degree of fun you might think has been missing from your life for a while.

6 WEDNESDAY *Moon Age Day 2   Moon Sign Aquarius*

This is a time during which gains come from fairly unexpected quarters. You don't feel the need to explain yourself to anyone but this could become something of a problem, especially at work. Even if you don't go into detail it would be good for others to know the way your mind is working.

Your Daily Guide to February 2019

7 THURSDAY   *Moon Age Day 3   Moon Sign Pisces*

Present trends tend to be particularly rewarding in terms of personal relationships though it might not look that way at the very start of the day. You are inclined to be rather withdrawn in a professional sense and probably will not be showing the best of yourself to the world in general today.

8 FRIDAY   *Moon Age Day 4   Moon Sign Pisces*

Don't jump to conclusions today. Instead, review the whole situation as thoroughly as you can before you take any action. Routines won't be of much interest and it is clear that you are attracted to whatever looks new and interesting. There could be some small financial gains later.

9 SATURDAY   *Moon Age Day 5   Moon Sign Aries*

This should be a pleasant weekend, particularly if you are in the company of people who make you feel happy. You won't be inclined to mix with those you find difficult or confusing and will be very selective about what you wish to do. This would be a really good day for a shopping spree.

10 SUNDAY   *Moon Age Day 6   Moon Sign Aries*

Although you can't run the show exactly as you would wish, it should still be possible to get your own way when it matters the most. This Sunday is a day during which you will want to ring the changes as much as possible and you certainly won't take kindly to others muscling in on what you consider to be your exclusive turf.

11 MONDAY   *Moon Age Day 7   Moon Sign Aries*

In some ways this could turn out to be a fairly unusual start to the week. There is a slight chance that mechanical things will be letting you down and it may be necessary to do certain jobs more than once in order to get them right. If you are short of ideas, ask a friend or colleague for help.

12 TUESDAY   *Moon Age Day 8   Moon Sign Taurus*

Prepare for minor setbacks and delays with regard to a certain project that is close to your heart today. Simply take these in your stride and don't be too worried about them. In the longer-term you know what you are doing and should be more than willing to follow a logical and sensible path.

Your Daily Guide to February 2019

13 WEDNESDAY
Moon Age Day 9   Moon Sign Taurus

The potential for the stars to bring new people into your life is now stronger than ever. You can't expect everyone you know to be equally helpful but the people who matter the most are more than willing to offer a sound point of view and some direct assistance. Plan now for an entertaining sort of weekend ahead.

14 THURSDAY
Moon Age Day 10   Moon Sign Gemini

You are no stranger to controversy, even though you don't actively invite it into your life. It is now very important to see the way others look at specific situations, if only so you have a yardstick by which to judge your own. Active and enterprising, you can turn an apparently dull day into a positive experience.

15 FRIDAY
Moon Age Day 11   Moon Sign Gemini

People gather round to see what you have to say today, so you should certainly not be lacking in attention. Enjoy your time in the spotlight. Aquarius is beginning to shine and it's a sight that is inclined to get you noticed. There is a great deal of fun on offer today, both for yourself and for those you care about.

16 SATURDAY
Moon Age Day 12   Moon Sign Cancer

With your high spirits and a good deal of enthusiasm it looks as though you are ready for anything that life throws your way. Not everyone will have your best interests at heart, especially in a professional sense, but you will know straight away if someone is trying to fool you in any way.

17 SUNDAY
Moon Age Day 13   Moon Sign Cancer

There are planetary aspects around now that allow you to take an issue that has troubled you for some time and to put it in the past for good. This is also an excellent time to bury the hatchet over a row that has been going on far too long. You should also be an excellent peacemaker to arbitrate between warring friends.

18 MONDAY
Moon Age Day 14   Moon Sign Leo

The lunar low is not likely to worry you very much this month. On the contrary, it seems as though you hardly recognise its presence. This is probably because there are quiet trends around in any case. You are hardly likely to be pushing over buses right now and will settle for a generally peaceful day.

Your Daily Guide to February 2019

19 TUESDAY
Moon Age Day 15   Moon Sign Leo

Don't expect it to be easy to get exactly what you want from life at the present time, especially in a financial sense. This could be a very family-oriented sort of day and a time during which you are restricting your activities for the sake of others. This particular trend won't last long at all.

20 WEDNESDAY
Moon Age Day 16   Moon Sign Virgo

Events at work could turn out to be slightly more profitable than you had been expecting. Apply yourself to whatever task seems to be most important but leave time later for having fun. The attitude of your partner takes some working out later in the day but turning on your usual Aquarian charm may help matters.

21 THURSDAY
Moon Age Day 17   Moon Sign Virgo

The focus right now is likely to be on romantic relationships, even though you are probably also very busy in a practical sense. You want to prove to the person you love the most just how important they are to your life and you should have little or no difficulty in doing so at any time today.

22 FRIDAY
Moon Age Day 18   Moon Sign Libra

There ought to be more power at your fingertips when it matters the most and with plenty of people around who are willing to go along with your ideas and to lend a hand, progress is more or less guaranteed. Your popularity is high and you may even be a little shocked about how many people want to know you better.

23 SATURDAY
Moon Age Day 19   Moon Sign Libra

Personal matters have more going for them than professional ones under present trends although, of course, to many Aquarians this is quite natural at the weekend. You want to find ways to have a good time and will also be in the right frame of mind to spoil your partner or family members. Later in the day you may get the chance to mix business with pleasure.

24 SUNDAY
Moon Age Day 20   Moon Sign Scorpio

An increase in your general level of luck can be expected around this time. This is likely to be especially true in the financial area of life but this is not a good time for gambling or taking too many chances. You will instinctively know when you can chance your arm – it's all a matter of intuition.

Your Daily Guide to February 2019

25 MONDAY *Moon Age Day 21   Moon Sign Scorpio*

You are likely to find yourself much more on the go in a general sense and won't have a great deal of time to please yourself at the moment. Never mind, you are getting a lot done and should be more than happy with your efforts before the end of the day. Friends should be very supportive.

26 TUESDAY *Moon Age Day 22   Moon Sign Sagittarius*

A family matter may come as a reminder of where you roots actually are. You will be very supportive of relatives and especially keen to give younger family members a hand if you can. Avoid getting involved in discussions that can have no logical conclusion because it would just be a waste of time.

27 WEDNESDAY *Moon Age Day 23   Moon Sign Sagittarius*

You certainly intend to be noticed at the moment and won't be taking a back seat in anything. The more arduous and demanding the task, the greater is your desire to succeed. Aquarius can be very sporting at this time but as in other areas of life you are a better team player than you are an individual champion.

28 THURSDAY *Moon Age Day 24   Moon Sign Sagittarius*

There could be an apparent decline in your fortunes but it really isn't anything to worry about. Difficult situations are temporary and you should not react to them more than is strictly necessary. Do a job today that you might normally have left until tomorrow because by that time you will be very busy again.

March 2019

Your Month at a Glance

⊕ = Opportunities are around   ⊖ = Be on the defensive   ● = Life is pretty ordinary

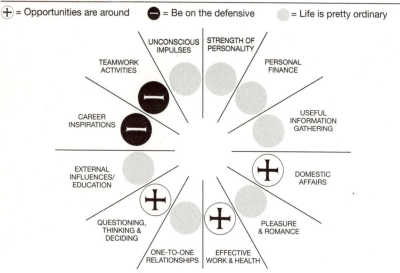

March Highs and Lows

Here I show you how the rhythms of the Moon will affect you this month. Like the tide, your energies and abilities will rise and fall with its pattern. When it is above the centre line, go for it, when it is below, you should be resting.

HIGH 3RD–5TH   **HIGH** 31ST   **LOW** 18TH–19TH

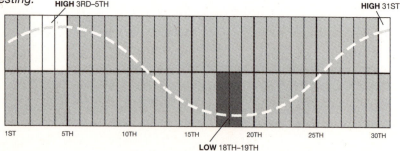

58

Your *Daily Guide to March 2019*

1 FRIDAY
Moon Age Day 25   Moon Sign Capricorn

There are gains and losses to be made today but the problem might lie in working out which is which. Not everything that starts out difficult remains so, whilst there are times today when blessings can turn rather sour. You need to be circumspect and even philosophical to get through this phase.

2 SATURDAY
Moon Age Day 26   Moon Sign Capricorn

There is now plenty of incentive to get on and do new things, freed from one or two of the restrictions that might have been around in the past. Friends are especially helpful and could offer you the chance to make more of yourself. This is an ideal time for mixing business with pleasure in some way.

3 SUNDAY
Moon Age Day 27   Moon Sign Aquarius

The lunar high brings the largest infusion of determination and drive that you have felt for a while You can push ahead progressively with your plans and desires and will discover that good luck is definitely on your side. Acting on impulse is a sure path to greater overall success now.

4 MONDAY
Moon Age Day 28   Moon Sign Aquarius

Hang rules and regulations! You make your own successes in your own way and won't be held back in the slightest by the way others want to do things. You are the major source of fun for the people you mix with today and will find ways to express yourself that surprise both you and those around you.

5 TUESDAY
Moon Age Day 29   Moon Sign Aquarius

In some respects you might only be part of the way along the road to where you really want to be but patience is one of your gifts and you can really show it at work today. The attitude of loved ones needs thinking about carefully, especially someone younger who seems to be going through a strange interlude.

6 WEDNESDAY ☿
Moon Age Day 0   Moon Sign Pisces

You will really enjoy being the centre of attention today and as a result, the level of your confidence increases noticeably. You aren't one to stay quiet in social situations and you once again have the ability to mix business with pleasure. Look out for some small financial gains.

Your Daily Guide to March 2019

7 THURSDAY ☿   *Moon Age Day 1   Moon Sign Pisces*

You can't expect everything to be exactly easy or smooth running at the moment but that won't bother you at all. You have great resilience at present and only really respect what you work hard to achieve. Some Aquarians will have the chance to take a journey soon and should grasp the opportunity with both hands.

8 FRIDAY ☿   *Moon Age Day 2   Moon Sign Aries*

Watch and wait because the time to strike is not quite here. There are hours around at the moment that were simply created for you to have fun. People come and go in your life at this time but there are a few stalwarts who will always be important to you. Show your loyalty to them today.

9 SATURDAY ☿   *Moon Age Day 3   Moon Sign Aries*

The place you most want to be right now is far from the madding crowd. This won't be possible all day but there ought to be interludes during which you can do whatever takes your fancy. The slower and more emotional responses of Aquarius are now fully in evidence and remain so for a few days.

10 SUNDAY ☿   *Moon Age Day 4   Moon Sign Taurus*

Keep a cool head today when it comes to putting your ideas across. It's a fine balance because too much excitement in your voice will lead others to wonder about you, while a lack of enthusiasm is also interpreted negatively. A certain degree of flexibility proves to be important today.

11 MONDAY ☿   *Moon Age Day 5   Moon Sign Taurus*

Social encounters can be fun at the start of a new working week and can even have a bearing on the way things are working out in a practical sense. Keep an open mind about changes that are offered to you in a professional sense. Not everything is quite what it appears to be today.

12 TUESDAY ☿   *Moon Age Day 6   Moon Sign Taurus*

You are already nearly half way through the month but you haven't made quite the progress you would have wished in a practical sense. There isn't too much you can do about this situation today, even though you register it. Instead of pushing to no end, instead simply find ways to have fun.

Your Daily Guide to March 2019

13 WEDNESDAY ☿ *Moon Age Day 7   Moon Sign Gemini*

Financial concerns could take the edge off this Wednesday if you allow them to. In reality, this is the sort of day on which you should shelve serious worries in favour of simply having a good time. There are exciting possibilities in the offing, particularly with regard to short journeys and even shopping trips.

14 THURSDAY ☿ *Moon Age Day 8   Moon Sign Gemini*

Someone you haven't seen for a while is likely to be returning to your life now. Welcome them with open arms and also enjoy what today has to offer in terms of change and diversity. Some Aquarians are only just waking up to the fact that this is a completely new year with fresh opportunities!

15 FRIDAY ☿ *Moon Age Day 9   Moon Sign Cancer*

Rules and regulations that get on the nerves of just about everyone else are easy for you to cope with right now. You are not lacking in confidence when you need it the most and this could allow you to make progress at work. By the evening you will probably be looking for something new to do in the company of those you admire.

16 SATURDAY ☿ *Moon Age Day 10   Moon Sign Cancer*

Today should be favourable for adventure and travel for all Aquarians. If, however, you are stuck in the daily grind, you can't expect to find every job easy to tackle but when it matters the most you will be getting on quite well. Keep in touch with people who are at a distance and do your best to impress if you are at work.

17 SUNDAY ☿ *Moon Age Day 11   Moon Sign Cancer*

You ought to be the life and soul of the party right now and though there are minor frustrations around early in the day none of these are likely to last very long. Some confusion over travel plans or the times of meetings needs to be addressed quickly but in most other respects things should be going well for you.

18 MONDAY ☿ *Moon Age Day 12   Moon Sign Leo*

The start of the working week can seem less positive than you would like, thanks to the arrival of the lunar low. Simply slow down a little and wait until circumstances improve before you try to get ahead in any way. It's only a matter of time before circumstances improve and there is nothing to prevent you from making plans until then.

Your Daily Guide to March 2019

19 TUESDAY ☿ *Moon Age Day 13   Moon Sign Leo*

Today might be rather quieter than you would have imagined but there's still room for instinct and intuition. You tend to be looking ahead now and won't be held back by too many complications. This is not an ideal time to take chances with money or love.

20 WEDNESDAY ☿ *Moon Age Day 14   Moon Sign Virgo*

There could be significant improvements where your professional goals are concerned and you should also find yourself in the right frame of mind to push ahead socially. There is plenty of energy around right now and you have a determination to see things through. Social trends are good towards the end of the day.

21 THURSDAY ☿ *Moon Age Day 15   Moon Sign Virgo*

You have a strong sense of your own ego that means making a definite impression. Not everyone is going to understand the more forceful side of your personality because it is clear right now that you are willing to make decisions. Others are used to you hedging your bets and a very certain Aquarian is something that is a little unusual.

22 FRIDAY ☿ *Moon Age Day 16   Moon Sign Libra*

Keep on the right side of those who are superior to you at work but do let them know that you are around. Your profile is high and the very likeable side of your nature is clearly on display. Don't get tied down with routines at the moment but stick to doing things you find interesting and stimulating.

23 SATURDAY ☿ *Moon Age Day 17   Moon Sign Libra*

In terms of money you should now be entering a fairly stable period. There are gains possibly coming from directions you didn't expect and you should also discover that your general earning power is greater than it might have been previously. There could be some special compliments coming your way this Saturday.

24 SUNDAY ☿ *Moon Age Day 18   Moon Sign Scorpio*

You tend to be very forthcoming and comfortable in your relationships, both the general ones and romantic ones. If you are at work it is important that you don't let your perception of your own limitations hold you back but instead believe that you are capable of anything. Along the way, you could easily surprise yourself.

Your Daily Guide to March 2019

25 MONDAY ☿ *Moon Age Day 19   Moon Sign Scorpio*

You can now deal very effectively with all professional matters, even if your home life suffers just a little as a result. There is plenty to be achieved this week and few interruptions to the general forward pace of your life. Keep up with local gossip and get involved in groups or associations.

26 TUESDAY ☿ *Moon Age Day 20   Moon Sign Sagittarius*

There ought to be a definite improvement to your romantic life around this time. In the practical world, however, there are likely to be annoying delays and a disturbance to your normal way of doing things. Be careful when dealing with mechanical gadgets, which might seem to be somewhat vindictive just now.

27 WEDNESDAY ☿ *Moon Age Day 21   Moon Sign Sagittarius*

Affairs of the heart bring the greatest satisfaction under present planetary trends. It is now easy for you to let your partner or sweetheart know how important they are to you and sweeping people off their feet ought to be a piece of cake. The attitude of friends might occasionally prove somewhat difficult however.

28 THURSDAY ☿ *Moon Age Day 22   Moon Sign Capricorn*

You tend to enjoy the company of others at this time and will be doing all you can to socialise, even if the pace of life is slightly slower than you might have wished. There are many distractions around at this time and concentrating fully on the tasks that lie before you is going to be far from easy.

29 FRIDAY *Moon Age Day 23   Moon Sign Capricorn*

This is a favourable period for all social activities and close relationships are particularly well-starred. There is a generally harmonious atmosphere around, both at work and at home. Make the most of the positive trends by asking for a favour or two and understand that friends are especially willing to help you now.

30 SATURDAY *Moon Age Day 24   Moon Sign Capricorn*

Examine your views regarding certain matters and ask yourself if you are being truly realistic. You are able to see through the haze that everyday life places over some issues and what you realise might surprise you. Enlist the support of relatives or friends if you find that you are out of your depth in any way.

Your Daily Guide to March 2019

31 SUNDAY
Moon Age Day 25   Moon Sign Aquarius

The lunar high brings some of the best potential situations you have experienced since the beginning of March. There are gains to be made in a financial sense, especially if you are willing to push your luck a little. Romance is also on the cards and some very positive encounters are the result of your sociability.

2019

Your Month at a Glance

⊕ = Opportunities are around   ⊖ = Be on the defensive   ● = Life is pretty ordinary

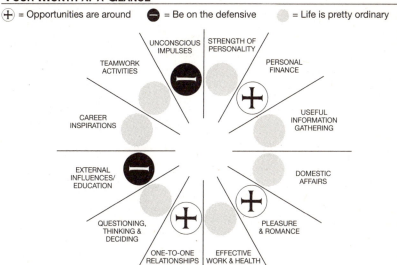

April Highs and Lows

Here I show you how the rhythms of the Moon will affect you this month. Like the tide, your energies and abilities will rise and fall with its pattern. When it is above the centre line, go for it, when it is below, you should be resting.

HIGH 1ST   HIGH 27TH–28TH

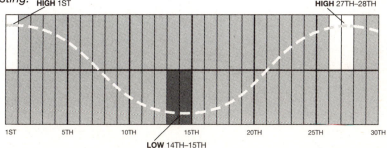

1ST   5TH   10TH   15TH   20TH   25TH   30TH

LOW 14TH–15TH

65

Your Daily Guide to April 2019

1 MONDAY   *Moon Age Day 26   Moon Sign Aquarius*

Getting your own way should be very easy at the moment and your silver tongue and natural cheek make it possible to bring reluctant colleagues or even family members round to your own point of view. There are arrangements to be made, quite possibly for a trip planned at very short notice.

2 TUESDAY   *Moon Age Day 27   Moon Sign Pisces*

There could be some slight confusion about at this stage of the week and you will have to be certain of details before pushing ahead with anything really important. There are slight gains to be made in the financial department but all in all you can expect to encounter a few obstacles.

3 WEDNESDAY   *Moon Age Day 28   Moon Sign Pisces*

Your confidence is not lacking when you find yourself undertaking tasks you fully understand and it is down this road you should be going today. Breaking new ground is fine and it's something you love to do but it doesn't lead to real success just at the moment. This could be a day of messages of one sort or another.

4 THURSDAY   *Moon Age Day 29   Moon Sign Pisces*

What a good time this is going to be for getting into the good books of others and for getting ahead in a professional and a financial way. You have had a few days that were good for planning and now you are likely to put what you have learned to good use. Friends prove to be very loyal.

5 FRIDAY   *Moon Age Day 0   Moon Sign Aries*

With a great zest for life generally, you should find that what you get from romantic clinches is now extremely promising and the full potential of April begins to show itself. It's not hard to make a good impression and you can put across a number of the excellent ideas that are occurring to you around this time.

6 SATURDAY   *Moon Age Day 1   Moon Sign Aries*

Creating the right atmosphere, either at work or at home, should appear to be very easy now and one of your greatest strengths is your ability to see how others are likely to behave in any given situation. This amounts to an almost psychic awareness that you should take full advantage of.

Your Daily Guide to April 2019

7 SUNDAY
Moon Age Day 2   Moon Sign Taurus

You clearly know what you want but getting it can prove to be quite a struggle if you insist on going it alone. It would be far better to rely on the ideas and opinions of friends and family members, many of whom have some excellent strategies for getting ahead. You are still looking for bright lights and good times.

8 MONDAY
Moon Age Day 3   Moon Sign Taurus

It looks as though you are seeking adventure and you will feel a great desire to be somewhere other than following the path of orthodoxy. Excitement is very appealing and at some time today you could be embarking on something that will lead to a completely new start.

9 TUESDAY
Moon Age Day 4   Moon Sign Gemini

Show some Aquarian patience and whilst not settling for second best, do what you can to accept your lot, if only for today. People you don't see all that often could well be making an appearance in your life at any time now and they have some interesting things to say.

10 WEDNESDAY
Moon Age Day 5   Moon Sign Gemini

There are likely to be a few financial ups and downs at this stage of the working week but Aquarians who are between jobs at present stand a good chance of hitting upon something new at any time. It is good to show the world what you know so don't be inclined to hide your light under a bushel.

11 THURSDAY
Moon Age Day 6   Moon Sign Gemini

Your confidence is at its strongest right now and this also means that you leave a good impression on others. In any situation it is good to strike whilst the iron is hot and to make the best of prevailing circumstances. Excitement is part of the package, even if the implications of your actions make you somewhat nervous.

12 FRIDAY
Moon Age Day 7   Moon Sign Cancer

Others will tell you that slow and steady wins the race. Sometimes that is true but it hardly applies to your life at the moment. On the contrary, you want to push ahead and to show the whole world how quickly you can arrive at your chosen destination. It is best to go with it and follow your instincts right now.

Your Daily Guide to April 2019

13 SATURDAY
Moon Age Day 8   Moon Sign Cancer

The act of taking the initiative is part of what being an Air-sign is all about and the planetary line-up now offers you new opportunities and a different way of assessing certain situations. Conforming to expectations won't always work and there are times now when it is good to surprise others a little.

14 SUNDAY
Moon Age Day 9   Moon Sign Leo

The restrictions brought about by the lunar low are in evidence in some spheres of your life but are far less likely to dog you in others. Try not to spend too much time dwelling on professional matters but rather concentrate on the social and romantic aspects of life in order to feel most comfortable now.

15 MONDAY
Moon Age Day 10   Moon Sign Leo

You might not be entirely comfortable with change right now and will be happier to deal with life as it has always been. That's fine for a short while and it won't do any harm to revel in nostalgia for now. Plan for later though, and tell yourself that what you are going through is nothing more than an interlude.

16 TUESDAY
Moon Age Day 11   Moon Sign Virgo

Places of entertainment are a must today. You need diversion and can find it in a host of different places. What wouldn't suit you at all right now would be to find yourself tied to a particular place or routine to the exclusion of all else. The most important thing today is to keep talking.

17 WEDNESDAY
Moon Age Day 12   Moon Sign Virgo

The more you mix with others, the greater is the amount of information that comes your way. You could be coming to the end of a particular incentive, which will leave you with more time to think up something new. People should be particularly helpful when it comes to work or financial matters.

18 THURSDAY
Moon Age Day 13   Moon Sign Libra

Most situations tend to be harmonious today and you may even consider that life is somewhat dull. If this turns out to be the case, you probably only have yourself to blame. In material matters and where decisions have to be made, take the bull by the horns. Your decision-making abilities are excellent now.

Your Daily Guide to April 2019

19 FRIDAY
Moon Age Day 14   Moon Sign Libra

Planetary trends move on, and now today you can expect setbacks when it comes to making decisions. The problem is likely to be that everyone has a different point of view and offers you alternative advice. It might be necessary to decide for yourself, even if one or two people directly disagree with your conclusions.

20 SATURDAY
Moon Age Day 15   Moon Sign Scorpio

Assistance arrives from unexpected places, especially when it comes to any issue involving money. Meanwhile, you show a very social face to the world and can get on well with everyone, even with people who haven't been your cup of tea in the past. Plan now for some sort of excursion later.

21 SUNDAY
Moon Age Day 16   Moon Sign Scorpio

Positive thinking can help you enormously at present. Even if you encounter the odd setback today, you will still be moving forward in a general sense. A growing desire to throw off the fetters of conventional thinking becomes apparent, though this is nothing too unusual for Aquarius.

22 MONDAY
Moon Age Day 17   Moon Sign Sagittarius

There are plenty of interesting things happening today, most probably associated with your love life. In addition, the very real effort that others put in on your behalf can make you feel generally good about yourself. Confidences offered to you at present must be carefully guarded.

23 TUESDAY
Moon Age Day 18   Moon Sign Sagittarius

You are likely to discover that it is impossible to please all of the people, all of the time today. Despite your acceptance of this fact, you are still likely to try to do so at some stage. How can you help it? Conciliation and arbitration are hallmarks of your zodiac sign. Just be prepared to encounter a number of awkward people around at the moment.

24 WEDNESDAY
Moon Age Day 19   Moon Sign Capricorn

Work and practical progress prove easy enough to deal with. Avoid allowing others to pressure you. This isn't too much of a problem now but might prove to be more so by the end of the week. Start as you mean to go on and let people know just how far you are willing to bend in any given situation.

Your Daily Guide to April 2019

25 THURSDAY
Moon Age Day 20   Moon Sign Capricorn

Loved ones seek emotional assistance and you should be in a good position to help them significantly. Aquarius is in a listening mood and so many of your efforts today are for the sake of those around you. Conforming to expectations in the workplace won't be all that easy, but you should try to do so.

26 FRIDAY
Moon Age Day 21   Moon Sign Capricorn

Restlessness could so easily pay you a visit now. In order to avoid this eventuality, you need to keep busy and to think up new schemes that you find both stimulating and potentially rewarding. The most entertaining people at the moment appear to be friends you have known for a long time.

27 SATURDAY
Moon Age Day 22   Moon Sign Aquarius

This is one of the best days of the month for getting your own way and the good news is that you won't have to bully anyone to do so. The lunar high keeps you charming and approachable, whilst at the same time displaying the natural dominance that makes others all too willing to fall in line with whatever you want.

28 SUNDAY
Moon Age Day 23   Moon Sign Aquarius

Self-belief is the name of the game today and the position of the Moon in your own zodiac sign is a great help. Keep faith with each of the decisions and moves you make. If you show a high level of confidence, it won't be long before you have more help than you could possibly need.

29 MONDAY
Moon Age Day 24   Moon Sign Pisces

Domestic matters require your individual attention and could turn out to be something of a chore. Younger family members, in particular, are quite demanding at a time when you really want to turn your attention to matters beyond your own door. Don't forget, patience is a virtue.

30 TUESDAY
Moon Age Day 25   Moon Sign Pisces

Though you could be caught up in personal issues, the events of today tend to be easy-going and generally pleasant. Perhaps you will become bored if this turns out to be the case. If so, you need to exercise a little self-discipline. Keep a sense of proportion regarding relationships of any sort.

May 2019

Your Month at a Glance

⊕ = Opportunities are around   ⊖ = Be on the defensive   ● = Life is pretty ordinary

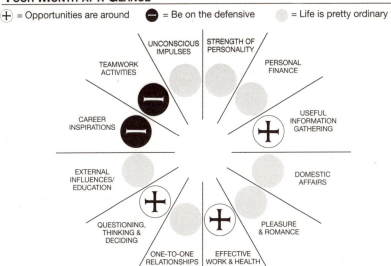

May Highs and Lows

Here I show you how the rhythms of the Moon will affect you this month. Like the tide, your energies and abilities will rise and fall with its pattern. When it is above the centre line, go for it, when it is below, you should be resting.

HIGH 24TH–26TH
LOW 11TH–12TH

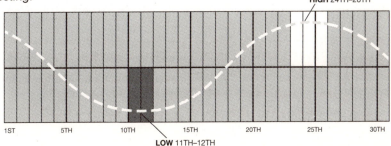

Your Daily Guide to May 2019

1 WEDNESDAY
Moon Age Day 26   Moon Sign Pisces

Pleasure may be high on your agenda today but that doesn't mean you lack the practical approach too. You will be better than anyone at organising others. Such is your present charisma that they are unlikely to go against you. All the same, listen to a contrary point of view because a mistake in judgement is not out of the question.

2 THURSDAY
Moon Age Day 27   Moon Sign Aries

This is a particularly good day to be out in the social mainstream and for enjoying the fruits of past labours. Some attention to detail where money is concerned may be necessary because it is likely you are spending more than is coming in. In the short-term, this won't matter but you will need to get your practical head on before long.

3 FRIDAY
Moon Age Day 28   Moon Sign Aries

Peace and quiet at home might not be much of an option today. This is not necessarily a bad thing however. It seems as though you have popularity on your side, which is why you are receiving so much attention and so many invitations. All the same, you can't do everything so some refusals may be necessary.

4 SATURDAY
Moon Age Day 0   Moon Sign Taurus

Don't put yourself under any more pressure than is strictly necessary at the moment. Your powers are not without limit and it is more than likely that you need a rest. Offload some jobs on to willing volunteers, especially at home, whilst you take just a short time out to think about things.

5 SUNDAY
Moon Age Day 1   Moon Sign Taurus

Almost everyone provides you with a friendly response this Sunday, so you should not have to try all that hard to achieve positive objectives. Leave material concerns on the shelf for the moment because present trends show you in the mood to have some fun. Friends contribute to a growing feeling of personal confidence.

6 MONDAY
Moon Age Day 2   Moon Sign Taurus

Emotional and domestic matters are now increasing your sense of security and belonging. If Aquarians feel snug and warm inside their own lives, outside matters tend to take care of themselves. Don't turn down a timely offer of assistance because to accept would not be a sign of failure.

Your Daily Guide to May 2019

7 TUESDAY *Moon Age Day 3   Moon Sign Gemini*

Under continuing positive trends for the family, relatives should have the ability to make you feel particularly warm and comfortable. Whether or not all of them choose to exercise this ability remains to be seen and is tied, in part, to your own attitude. Certainly in the case of younger relatives, you may need to offer incentives that imply trust.

8 WEDNESDAY *Moon Age Day 4   Moon Sign Gemini*

Put a few responsibilities to one side today while you sit back and decide to have some fun. Although you might be somewhat concerned at the behaviour of your partner or perhaps a good friend, you should be able to take the people concerned out of themselves – a remedy for almost any ill.

9 THURSDAY *Moon Age Day 5   Moon Sign Cancer*

You will be happy today if you can make room for personal indulgences. Aquarius doesn't usually go in for a life of luxury but it is good to spoil yourself once in a while. By the middle of the day, some of that irrepressible energy makes an appearance and you will be joining in with whatever needs doing.

10 FRIDAY *Moon Age Day 6   Moon Sign Cancer*

Though the pace of events is hurried, particularly at work, you will still find the time to socialise and to give your personal life an overhaul in some respects. You may benefit from some lovely compliments coming your way at present, though you will have to pay attention if you don't want to miss them.

11 SATURDAY *Moon Age Day 7   Moon Sign Leo*

Whatever you decide to take on board today, remember that your energy level isn't all that high. It might be best to stay out of the limelight and to spend as many hours as you can doing something quiet. Personal relationships should be going well and will be broadly unaffected by the lunar low.

12 SUNDAY *Moon Age Day 8   Moon Sign Leo*

Another generally quiet sort of day and certainly not one during which you should take on jobs you know will be contentious or difficult. There is plenty of time tomorrow to get on with whatever you wish but for the moment be content to stay in company you know, avoiding unnecessary risks.

Your Daily Guide to May 2019

13 MONDAY
Moon Age Day 9   Moon Sign Virgo

You show a natural curiosity and a real desire to broaden your horizons. This means you find yourself with another day that responds well to changes of scenery. Give and take proves to be important in personal matters but you will always get your own way in the end, and without upsetting any apple carts.

14 TUESDAY
Moon Age Day 10   Moon Sign Virgo

There could be pressures coming along in your social life, mainly born of boredom if you have to do the same old things. It's time to ring the changes, even though to do so won't please everyone. The individualist within you has to show its face as soon as possible.

15 WEDNESDAY
Moon Age Day 11   Moon Sign Libra

The emphasis today is definitely on the domestic scene, so you may choose not to travel too far on this late spring Wednesday. Everything points to your private life being positively highlighted and many Aquarians will be in a position to enjoy the fruits of their love life at the moment.

16 THURSDAY
Moon Age Day 12   Moon Sign Libra

You can probably hope for a more fulfilling period than you have experienced for a little while. Whether you are actually getting on any better remains in doubt because what has changed is only your state of mind. The planets now bring a strong boost to your confidence and a greater sense of personal determination.

17 FRIDAY
Moon Age Day 13   Moon Sign Scorpio

Decision-making at work tends to turn out much more successfully than you might imagine. You are now in a far better position to influence situations and will have what it takes to get on-side with those who pull the strings of life. You won't like routine today and tend to cherry-pick the most interesting tasks.

18 SATURDAY
Moon Age Day 14   Moon Sign Scorpio

This would be a superb time to entertain at home, though you also have what it takes to make a good impression out there in the big wide world. The only problem at the moment is that you could be stuck for choice and what you don't want is to take on so much you do nothing properly.

Your Daily Guide to May 2019

19 SUNDAY   *Moon Age Day 15   Moon Sign Scorpio*

Divide your time equally between social matters and cultural pursuits. That way you get the best from both worlds. Also remember that some types of excitement don't last very long so you are best off opting for a more settled sort of fun. Supporting those who care about you is probably closest to your heart at present.

20 MONDAY   *Moon Age Day 16   Moon Sign Sagittarius*

You may be in danger of overlooking some important details today, and you could be forgiven for believing that certain elements of your life are just slightly out of control. Stop and take stock because most of the situations towards which you are presently rushing can wait a while if necessary.

21 TUESDAY   *Moon Age Day 17   Moon Sign Sagittarius*

It will seem that the domestic sphere is where you want to be the most at the moment. That doesn't mean you have to be tied to your home, though, and it is likely that you will be escaping with the family at some point. Your partner should be especially supportive at the moment, especially if you decide on a heart-to-heart talk.

22 WEDNESDAY   *Moon Age Day 18   Moon Sign Capricorn*

At work you may experience some minor irritations that you can't do much about. Avoid making long-term decisions and be willing to wait and see in most situations. The more routine your life becomes at this time, the better you are likely to cope because excitement is not on the agenda, at least for now.

23 THURSDAY   *Moon Age Day 19   Moon Sign Capricorn*

There is now a very positive slant on all matters associated with communication. If you have to speak in public around this time you should do so with great confidence and success. Not everyone gathers to laud your skill, but those who don't might well be suffering from a little jealousy.

24 FRIDAY   *Moon Age Day 20   Moon Sign Aquarius*

This is the best time of the month for making new starts and for taking chances of almost any sort. People instantly recognise your potential, which means lots of people surrounding you and a high degree of popularity. Any recent fog of confusion tends to be blown away by the power of today's lunar high.

Your Daily Guide to May 2019

25 SATURDAY
Moon Age Day 21   Moon Sign Aquarius

Today seeks a physical and mental peak for most people born under the zodiac sign of Aquarius. This means new opportunities and brings extra impetus to old ones. Hardly anyone could doubt your present commitment or your positive frame of mind. The world contributes to some of your successes now, but most of the effort is down to you.

26 SUNDAY
Moon Age Day 22   Moon Sign Aquarius

You can make a positive impact on the right people at the moment and will still be cruising quite well through your life. Loyalty is an important consideration to you at any time, but especially at the moment. Those who know you best are now much more likely to call on your unconditional support.

27 MONDAY
Moon Age Day 23   Moon Sign Pisces

A work issue could be the cause of some frustration early in the day and you would be well advised to get things sorted out as quickly as possible. People you haven't known all that well in the past may begin to play a more important role in your life and you will be more than ready to form some new friendships.

28 TUESDAY
Moon Age Day 24   Moon Sign Pisces

You have a desire to break the bounds of the conventional and to spread your wings in some way. What an excellent period this would be for a hastily arranged holiday or simply a day or two away. Everything seems fresh and somehow more real under the current planetary trends, so make the most of this time.

29 WEDNESDAY
Moon Age Day 25   Moon Sign Aries

As your ego seems to be growing by the minute, there is a potential danger of being too pushy for your own good today. Sticking with convention is never really your thing and the more outrageous side of your personality is now clearly on display. Rather than disapproving, however, others find you fascinating.

30 THURSDAY
Moon Age Day 26   Moon Sign Aries

There is a positive boost coming in terms of your professional life, even if this takes a little while to make itself known. You might have to put in that extra bit of effort that can make all the difference and you certainly won't be worried about ruffling a few feathers if that is what it takes to get ahead.

Your Daily Guide to May 2019

31 FRIDAY

Moon Age Day 27   Moon Sign Aries

Social contacts should be both exciting and helpful and there is a good spark to your character at the moment that fascinates others. Try not to take on too much in a practical sense but rather find ways to have fun. The powerful influence of a loved one makes itself felt in your life around this time.

2019

Your Month at a Glance

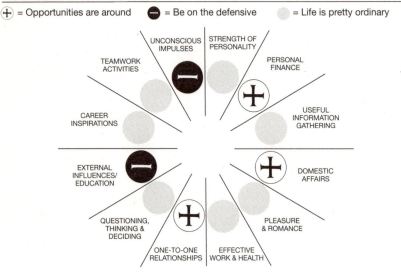

June Highs and Lows

Here I show you how the rhythms of the Moon will affect you this month. Like the tide, your energies and abilities will rise and fall with its pattern. When it is above the centre line, go for it, when it is below, you should be resting.

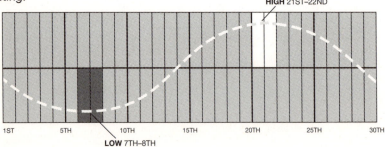

Your Daily Guide to June 2019

1 SATURDAY *Moon Age Day 28   Moon Sign Taurus*

Practical matters can put some strain on you at the moment and it is very important to realise that a little patience can go a long way. This would not be a good day to shoot from the hip or to wage war with yourself just because things are not going right. Take some time out to smell the roses.

2 SUNDAY *Moon Age Day 29   Moon Sign Taurus*

Though you may be rather sluggish at first, this should be a good day for problem solving. You are able to sit down and work things out well beyond the ability of those around you. With plenty of zest for life developing as the day goes one, this is the start of a positive interlude that lasts a couple of days.

3 MONDAY *Moon Age Day 0   Moon Sign Gemini*

Life should be going rather well for you now and the only thing you need to avoid today is spur of the moment decisions or making purchases that you simply don't need. There are times when it is necessary to tell someone the way things really are and you could find that to be the case by this evening.

4 TUESDAY *Moon Age Day 1   Moon Sign Gemini*

Personal and emotional issues may well take precedence over practical matters at times today but you are likely to be full of beans and anxious to get on with your life in a big way. Maybe this conflict could lead to a little frustration, especially if your partner or family members are demanding too much of you right now.

5 WEDNESDAY *Moon Age Day 2   Moon Sign Cancer*

Perhaps you feel the need to introduce a little variety into your life today? You should be inspirational, entertaining and extremely interesting to others. Unfortunately, though, as you make such a good impression, everyone wants your attention at the same time. Don't expect it to be easy to get on with what you want to do as a result.

6 THURSDAY *Moon Age Day 3   Moon Sign Cancer*

Lots of personal reassurance and a greater sense of fulfilment are coming your way through today's trends. Get to grips with matters in the family and share ideas about new projects with friends – you should find they are interested. Your confidence in your ability to do what you think is right grows as the day moves on.

Your Daily Guide to June 2019

7 FRIDAY
Moon Age Day 4   Moon Sign Leo

Keep your material sights low for the weekend ahead because if you do the lunar low will hardly touch your life at all this time round. The less you bother yourself with financial considerations, the greater is going to be the joy you get from relationships and from having the sort of fun that won't cost you a bean.

8 SATURDAY
Moon Age Day 5   Moon Sign Leo

Right now planetary influences don't appear to be doing you too many favours but as long as you are in the bosom of your family, or involved with really good friends, you won't mind this at all. True, you will settle for a slower pace of life but that simply means you take more notice of all that is happening around you as summer unfolds.

9 SUNDAY
Moon Age Day 6   Moon Sign Virgo

Compartmentalise your time carefully and allow someone else to take a little of the strain today. Unexpected duties and obligations now tend to distract you from your desire to get on with specific personal tasks. This is going to delay things somewhat but it should not prevent you from spending at least some time on yourself.

10 MONDAY
Moon Age Day 7   Moon Sign Virgo

Although you won't feel particularly daring today, there are people around who can convince you that taking the odd risk can be fun. Don't walk away from a challenge right now and be willing to look at any new option in an open-minded way. Money matters should be looking better by the end of the day.

11 TUESDAY
Moon Age Day 8   Moon Sign Virgo

There is plenty of capture your attention today, though at least some of it might not be relevant to your life. Look out for potential financial gains and be patient regarding a long-term project that can only mature when the circumstances are right. In the meantime, find ways to have fun with family and friends.

12 WEDNESDAY
Moon Age Day 9   Moon Sign Libra

Apply yourself to the task of inventing new strategies as much and as often as you can on this Wednesday. You are still in the mood to get ahead and you should find a wealth of people around who are more than willing to lend you a hand. Romance is in the air for young or young-at-heart Aquarians – which is potentially all of you.

Your Daily Guide to June 2019

13 THURSDAY *Moon Age Day 10   Moon Sign Libra*

Stand by, Aquarius, because this can be quite a startling day, just as long as you handle it right from the start. Get on with what pleases you and do everything to the very best of your ability. There are plenty of opportunities to shine when in company and you may well discover that you are flavour of the month at work.

14 FRIDAY *Moon Age Day 11   Moon Sign Scorpio*

Your energy is still reasonably high so you should have little difficulty getting through most of the tasks you set yourself today. It is important that you avoid trying to bite off more than you can chew and it would be sensible to take frequent breaks. The real problem might be getting bored with routines, so ring the changes.

15 SATURDAY *Moon Age Day 12   Moon Sign Scorpio*

There should be good results coming along in the practical sphere on a Saturday that has much going for it in terms of getting things done on a concrete level. Nebulous thoughts and little worries can be dismissed because actions are what matter right now. Your confidence in those closest to you is likely to increase markedly.

16 SUNDAY *Moon Age Day 13   Moon Sign Sagittarius*

Exciting social encounters can be expected today. Stay away from what you see as being pointless rules and regulations because these will only annoy you. Friends should prove to be both supportive and interesting as the day wears on. You have strength of personality now and you will not retreat from any challenge.

17 MONDAY *Moon Age Day 14   Moon Sign Sagittarius*

Aquarius can be the life and soul of the party at the moment. Although you might not be making the forward strides you would wish in the workplace, you will be able to compensate for this fact by using your natural charm. It is not necessary to bulldoze your way through any obstacle now.

18 TUESDAY *Moon Age Day 15   Moon Sign Capricorn*

A heavily competitive element comes along now, forcing you to look at even existing circumstances in a radically different way. You won't want to lose at any game or sport, whilst in terms of your career prospects your mind is working overtime. All the same, find a few hours to enjoy yourself.

Your Daily Guide to June 2019

19 WEDNESDAY *Moon Age Day 16   Moon Sign Capricorn*

Despite your best efforts, it could now appear that you are missing out somehow in the career stakes. This would be an ideal time for a reappraisal. If necessary, seek out some professional advice and certainly don't assume that you already know the answer to any problem.

20 THURSDAY *Moon Age Day 17   Moon Sign Capricorn*

Success comes at the moment partly from being well organised. You can fall down only if you haven't dealt with all eventualities. Don't let opportunities slip by simply because you haven't prepared yourself properly. This would be a good time to instigate new business partnerships.

21 FRIDAY *Moon Age Day 18   Moon Sign Aquarius*

This is a day for going for what you want, even if there are people around who wish to prevent you from doing so. You know your own mind best and whilst the lunar high is around you must make full use of all new possibilities. At work you should be really showing that you are a force to be reckoned with.

22 SATURDAY *Moon Age Day 19   Moon Sign Aquarius*

The lunar high supports your efforts in a number of directions and allows a higher degree of luck to come your way. In reality, it is possible that you are making most of your present luck as you go along. The only slight problem is a tendency to rush things rather more than will turn out to be good for you.

23 SUNDAY *Moon Age Day 20   Moon Sign Pisces*

It is possible that you will discover other people's true feelings about you around this time. In the main, you ought to be delighted but your ego can easily be dented if not all responses are exactly as you would wish. You may need to come to terms with the fact that not everyone loves you.

24 MONDAY *Moon Age Day 21   Moon Sign Pisces*

If financial stability is on your mind right now you could find ways and means to improve the situation. You may need to follow up on a couple of leads and perhaps to read some printed matter. However, with a good deal of thought and a little action, finances could look very much stronger before long.

Your Daily Guide to June 2019

25 TUESDAY
Moon Age Day 22   Moon Sign Pisces

A successful time can be expected in affairs of the heart, whether these are lifelong or simply casual relationships. It won't be easy to conforming to the expectations that certain family members have of you, and you may need to be tolerant, particularly when dealing with younger people.

26 WEDNESDAY
Moon Age Day 23   Moon Sign Aries

There is plenty of energy present at the moment to allow you to break through barriers that might have looked high and wide indeed in the recent past. You might be left wondering why you were intimidated in the first place and you will definitely be sharpening your persuasive skills and general intellect today.

27 THURSDAY
Moon Age Day 24   Moon Sign Aries

Romantic affairs continue to be positively highlighted, though now the trends are better with regard to long-term commitments. Keep an open mind regarding the ideas and opinions of certain family members, one or two of whom could have been causing you headaches for some time.

28 FRIDAY
Moon Age Day 25   Moon Sign Taurus

In relationships, you are not as friendly and giving today as has been the case recently. Perhaps it is the competitive side of your nature that is on display but for one reason or another it is harder to get close to specific people. With the weekend in view, you should be planning now for a change of scenery.

29 SATURDAY
Moon Age Day 26   Moon Sign Taurus

Though your dealings with others in social settings could be somewhat strained, there are those amongst your friends who rate you highly. Practically speaking, this is a time of high achievement. Avoid unnecessary discussions about situations that don't interest you and which you cannot alter.

30 SUNDAY
Moon Age Day 27   Moon Sign Gemini

There are plenty of opportunities to hog the limelight, though you may be tiring of having to smile so much. You won't be stuck for an answer and this is definitely the best time for putting yourself on display. If there are any limitations on you during present trends, these are probably self-created.

July 2019

YOUR MONTH AT A GLANCE

⊕ = Opportunities are around   ⊖ = Be on the defensive   ● = Life is pretty ordinary

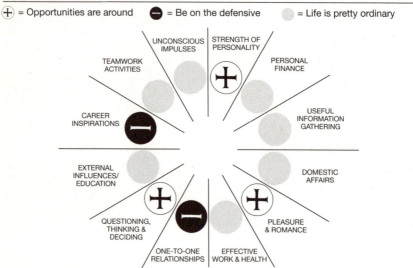

JULY HIGHS AND LOWS

Here I show you how the rhythms of the Moon will affect you this month. Like the tide, your energies and abilities will rise and fall with its pattern. When it is above the centre line, go for it, when it is below, you should be resting.

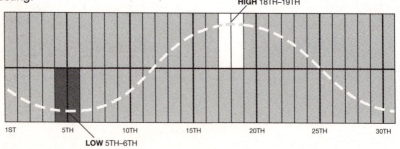

HIGH 18TH–19TH
LOW 5TH–6TH

Your Daily Guide to July 2019

1 MONDAY
Moon Age Day 28   Moon Sign Gemini

You now find yourself in a period during which all practical matters should push ahead quite nicely. Difficulties associated with relationships are less likely at this time and you can rely on friends to offer the sort of support you need when you want it the most. This should be a good start to the week.

2 TUESDAY
Moon Age Day 0   Moon Sign Gemini

Your good ideas and ingenuity are called into play this week. People you might never have suspected of keeping in touch with your opinions will be sounding you out now and might also offer you something in return. Romance looks fine too, maybe with a surprise or two on the way.

3 WEDNESDAY
Moon Age Day 1   Moon Sign Cancer

There is a definite tendency towards acquisition at this stage of the week and this might cause you to focus on the wrong things. Whilst you can make money in one way, it is likely to be slipping through your fingers in others. You don't lack confidence, but you will still need to concentrate hard.

4 THURSDAY
Moon Age Day 2   Moon Sign Cancer

Socialising looks good today, though not if you allow yourself to get involved in disputes that shouldn't be taking place at all. Try to remain neutral, even playing arbitrator amongst arguing friends. The subject might be interesting but you must steer a careful course if you don't want to be drawn into trouble.

5 FRIDAY
Moon Age Day 3   Moon Sign Leo

Although today should be happy and generally content, it might not be all that eventful. You can thank the lunar low for this state of affairs but you don't have to allow it to push you down into the doldrums. Get a change of scene, put on your best clothes and rely on friends to make the running.

6 SATURDAY
Moon Age Day 4   Moon Sign Leo

Give and take proves to be important in very personal relationships and you should steer clear of showing any sort of jealousy, which will only cause others to become angry. Even if you are a very young and inexperienced Aquarian you need to show a degree of maturity in matters of the heart.

Your Daily Guide to July 2019

7 SUNDAY
Moon Age Day 5   Moon Sign Virgo

There is danger right now in trying to make the world run the way you wish. It would be far better for the moment to realise that your own opinions belong to you and that others may not share them. Mistakes will be made today but luckily you are good at loss limitation exercises.

8 MONDAY ☿
Moon Age Day 6   Moon Sign Virgo

This is likely to be a better day for most sons and daughters of Aquarius. There have been quite a few potential complications about, though the fog clears as the new week commences. Confidential remarks made to you right now need to be treated very carefully. Under no circumstances should you spill the beans.

9 TUESDAY ☿
Moon Age Day 7   Moon Sign Libra

When it comes to getting what you want, you are king of the castle this week. Of all the working weeks of July, this one should be potentially the best. Although you might find it difficult to understand what makes loved ones tick, you are not having anywhere near the same problem with either colleagues or friends.

10 WEDNESDAY ☿
Moon Age Day 8   Moon Sign Libra

Material gains were never going to be far away during a period in which you are registering so many personal successes. You remain confident, and now you become something of a diplomat. Warring parties in any sphere of your life are treated to a dose of your ability to act as an intermediary.

11 THURSDAY ☿
Moon Age Day 9   Moon Sign Scorpio

You are out to impress people today and it won't be hard to do so. Conforming to expectations won't be all that easy, mainly because you are a born original in the first place. Your creative potential is good and you might spend at least part of today somehow brightening up your home surroundings.

12 FRIDAY ☿
Moon Age Day 10   Moon Sign Scorpio

Your mind is of the quick-fire variety today and you won't be stuck for an answer, no matter what the question might be. This doesn't mean to say that all your comments are either correct or very clever, but you can fool enough people to get by well enough. A little cheek goes a long way.

Your Daily Guide to July 2019

13 SATURDAY ☿   *Moon Age Day 11   Moon Sign Sagittarius*

Specific information that comes to you now from colleagues or possibly friends is definitely worth listening to carefully. Don't assume you have all the answers yourself and do be willing to admit your limitations. If you ally the skills of those around you to your own, the sky is the limit.

14 SUNDAY ☿   *Moon Age Day 12   Moon Sign Sagittarius*

Don't take no for an answer in situations about which you are absolutely certain – but at the same time avoid treading on any toes by exercising some diplomacy. Not everyone is equally easy to deal with, so you will need to listen carefully to what others have to say before you speak out.

15 MONDAY ☿   *Moon Age Day 13   Moon Sign Capricorn*

Even though you know what you are doing, the same cannot be said to be true of people with whom you have to co-operate. It would be sensible to check and double check almost anything now, particularly documents that always require scrutiny. Aquarius cannot leave anything to chance now.

16 TUESDAY ☿   *Moon Age Day 14   Moon Sign Capricorn*

You might be quite tired of doing things the same old way all the time and will be quite anxious to make changes wherever possible. Being the sort of person you are it should be quite easy to enlist some support and to get people on your side. Routines are definitely for the birds today, so ignore them when you can.

17 WEDNESDAY ☿   *Moon Age Day 15   Moon Sign Capricorn*

Things might turn out entirely differently from the way you intended, but don't take this to mean that situations are working out to your disadvantage. Nothing could be further from the truth. The fact is that you are good at thinking on your feet and that you can turn an apparent problem into a very positive blessing.

18 THURSDAY ☿   *Moon Age Day 16   Moon Sign Aquarius*

Today finds the Moon returning to your zodiac sign, leading to a period of high activity and a time that revolves around your social life. There might not be all that many hours for practicalities but since you have charm galore, you can get others to do the dirty work while you please yourself.

Your Daily Guide to July 2019

19 FRIDAY ☿   *Moon Age Day 17   Moon Sign Aquarius*

There is positive help around when you need it today, which may bolster your personally held view that you know your business best. The desire for a change of scene could be very strong and is emphasised even more by the lunar high. What an excellent time this would be for Aquarius to take a holiday.

20 SATURDAY ☿   *Moon Age Day 18   Moon Sign Pisces*

Personal relationships need an extra boost and this can only really come from your direction. Be willing to pay a few compliments and don't leave people in the dark when it comes to arrangements that have a bearing on their lives. Aquarius needs to be very open and honest at present.

21 SUNDAY ☿   *Moon Age Day 19   Moon Sign Pisces*

Don't commit yourself to mundane tasks now but rather go out and get what you really want from life. You often like to act on impulse, but this trait is much enhanced today. Aquarians of all ages should now find that the level of their popularity with others is going off the scale.

22 MONDAY ☿   *Moon Age Day 20   Moon Sign Pisces*

Enjoy what life has to offer but remember once again that you achieve the most now when you complete every job before beginning the next. You keep travelling the smooth path towards your objectives and can gain a great deal from simply being in the right place at the right time. The Sun is particularly helpful around now.

23 TUESDAY ☿   *Moon Age Day 21   Moon Sign Aries*

You could find others to be slightly more assertive than you might wish today and that means having to gauge your own responses pretty carefully. Although you won't want to upset people you might have to rely on eventually, you won't put up with any nonsense at present. Take care that this stance does not lead to a slight problem or two.

24 WEDNESDAY ☿   *Moon Age Day 22   Moon Sign Aries*

This is a good period for all types of relationships. The reason is that the Sun has now moved into your solar seventh house, which is positive from a number of different angles. Those you are close to romantically now respond to you instinctively, and react very positively to the attention you give them.

Your Daily Guide to July 2019

25 THURSDAY   ☿   *Moon Age Day 23   Moon Sign Taurus*

You clearly have some ingenious ideas up your sleeve around now and won't be at all shy about sharing them with the people who really count. Working out exactly who this might be won't be quite as easy as you may think but it's likely that your gut reactions are worth following at this time.

26 FRIDAY   ☿   *Moon Age Day 24   Moon Sign Taurus*

You should be very assertive today and that counts. It may be that in reality you are not half as assured as you appear to be, but that doesn't matter. When it comes to pleasing others you seem to have exactly what it takes now and can bend your nature to suit whatever circumstances and people come along.

27 SATURDAY   ☿   *Moon Age Day 25   Moon Sign Taurus*

You may prefer to avoid ambitious go-getting this weekend. This isn't a problem because you have achieved a good deal across the last few days and genuinely deserve a break now. In matters of the heart you will be quite instinctive in your reactions and will usually find the answers you need.

28 SUNDAY   ☿   *Moon Age Day 26   Moon Sign Gemini*

This is a time when romance is highlighted more favourably than at any period this month. All the more reason to take notice when someone tells you they think you are very special. Although you might be inclined to shrug off compliments, in all probability the people concerned are in earnest.

29 MONDAY   ☿   *Moon Age Day 27   Moon Sign Gemini*

Discussions may be marred by people who won't take anything seriously and it is very important to make it plain from the word go that you will not be messed about. Once you have put forward an entirely reasonable point of view, you will have to sit back and see how things develop. Don't be too quick to judge a friend.

30 TUESDAY   ☿   *Moon Age Day 28   Moon Sign Cancer*

It is very important that you broaden your horizons in some ways now. Do whatever you can to open yourself up to the wider world and don't turn away any reasonable offer of more responsibility. Although some sorts of advancement might seem to be quite intimidating, you are clearly up to the challenge.

31 WEDNESDAY ☿

Moon Age Day 0   Moon Sign Cancer

Although it is clear that not everyone has your best interests at heart, the people who matter the most to you couldn't be more helpful. Avoid a little tedium by convincing someone else to cope with the routines, particularly at home. That should leave you free to pursue a few dreams of your own invention.

2019

Your Month at a Glance

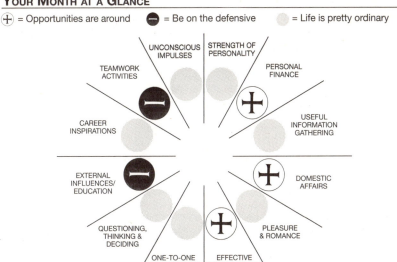

+ = Opportunities are around   − = Be on the defensive   ● = Life is pretty ordinary

August Highs and Lows

Here I show you how the rhythms of the Moon will affect you this month. Like the tide, your energies and abilities will rise and fall with its pattern. When it is above the centre line, go for it, when it is below, you should be resting.

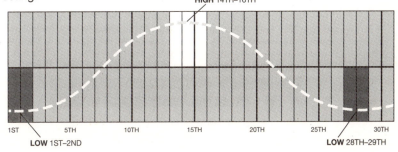

HIGH 14TH–16TH
LOW 1ST–2ND
LOW 28TH–29TH

Your Daily Guide to August 2019

1 THURSDAY
Moon Age Day 1   Moon Sign Leo

Keeping a low profile would be most sensible for the next couple of days. After a hectic period the lunar low comes along, sapping your strength and making it rather more difficult to see ahead of yourself. There's no harm in taking stock now and again and that is what this period is all about.

2 FRIDAY
Moon Age Day 2   Moon Sign Leo

You would be better off hanging fire on important decisions, even if this means telling a few white lies. You need to be very sure that anything you decide for the future is going to be in your best interests and that won't be easy at the moment. Your creative potential remains good so find other ways to stay happy.

3 SATURDAY
Moon Age Day 3   Moon Sign Virgo

Focus on personal relationships today and don't forget to put that extra bit of effort into them that can make all the difference. You don't want anyone feeling left out, so it is important to try especially hard to show your concern and affection. Friends, in particular, will be grateful for your presence.

4 SUNDAY
Moon Age Day 4   Moon Sign Virgo

Those higher up the tree in some way might oppose you at present, possibly because you are asking questions that make them rather uneasy. It might be prudent to back off a little rather than cause yourself problems further down the line, but you certainly won't do so if you think you are being sold short or duped.

5 MONDAY
Moon Age Day 5   Moon Sign Libra

Your home environment is likely to be very fulfilling around now. This is an excellent period during which to relive the past in some way, whilst at the same time putting a new slant on old situations. Friends you haven't seen for quite a while are likely to come out of the woodwork, bringing nostalgic feelings.

6 TUESDAY
Moon Age Day 6   Moon Sign Libra

Twosomes and joint endeavours of all kinds will appeal to you under present trends and your ability to co-operate is even more noteworthy than usual. The quirky side of your nature begins to show more but this is part of what makes you so attractive. Even when your confidence isn't especially high, nobody would guess.

Your Daily Guide to August 2019

7 WEDNESDAY   *Moon Age Day 7   Moon Sign Scorpio*

Almost everyone should now find you to be engaging and charming, which means you have even more influence than you had before. You won't mind being the leader of the pack when it comes to group activities of one sort or another and you are up for an adventure or two before today is out.

8 THURSDAY   *Moon Age Day 8   Moon Sign Scorpio*

There is a stronger emphasis today on the fun you can have with others. It seems as though practically everyone wants to be your friend and making the best sort of impression in almost any situation will be child's play. It might be later in the day before you realise how well you are actually doing.

9 FRIDAY   *Moon Age Day 9   Moon Sign Sagittarius*

It is quite possible that major changes are about to overtake you – not that this proves to be much of a problem because of all the zodiac signs you are the one that is most likely to take such situations in your stride. This Friday has variable trends but works best when you spend time doing things that appeal to you personally.

10 SATURDAY   *Moon Age Day 10   Moon Sign Sagittarius*

Your love life seems to provide your best moments this weekend. Although you are likely to be busy enough, it is when you are alone with the one you care about the most that the magic really starts. Your mood now is electric and you won't have any trouble impressing almost anyone.

11 SUNDAY   *Moon Age Day 11   Moon Sign Sagittarius*

Exchanges of opinion are important now, but don't go over the top because you can be very powerful and might be accused of bulldozing through your ideas and opinions. Instead of talking all the time, take time out to listen. You will still get your way in the end but do so in the considered, kind way that typifies your zodiac sign.

12 MONDAY   *Moon Age Day 12   Moon Sign Capricorn*

Right now you enjoy the best possible trends as far as your social life is concerned. You want to get on well with everyone but may have to ignore the odd awkward type who crosses your path. This stage of the month will bring its own concerns but these are not of the sort that will hold you back in any way.

Your Daily Guide to August 2019

13 TUESDAY *Moon Age Day 13   Moon Sign Capricorn*

As a result of the effort you have put in during the last few weeks, you should be seeing the fruit of your endeavours at any time now. It is possible you will be slightly better off and life is likely to appear more settled in some way. If things are too quiet you can be relied upon to find ways to make it topsy-turvy again.

14 WEDNESDAY *Moon Age Day 14   Moon Sign Aquarius*

Don't miss out on upcoming news because you will learn plenty that you will want to know. After a quieter day yesterday the lunar high comes thundering into your life, giving you greater energy and thrusting you like a rocket into the centre of all that is happening around you. You tend to make up your own rules today.

15 THURSDAY *Moon Age Day 15   Moon Sign Aquarius*

You achieve a physical peak today and should be happy to take on extra work without even feeling you are doing so. With everything to play for in a personal sense, you now have what it takes to impress someone. The level of your charm is even higher than usual and you should be feeling good about life generally.

16 FRIDAY *Moon Age Day 16   Moon Sign Aquarius*

Financial planning undertaken now is likely to work out well. You have a very astute head on your shoulders and are also in a good position to see a host of different possibilities and strategies around this time. Aquarius is both confident and comfortable at the moment, and it shows.

17 SATURDAY *Moon Age Day 17   Moon Sign Pisces*

Although it is clear you are looking for a high degree of personal freedom right now, you must get important jobs out of the way before you think about taking a break. Don't be inclined to sit on the fence in issues you know to be important. Even if it means disagreeing with a friend, you have to speak your mind.

18 SUNDAY *Moon Age Day 18   Moon Sign Pisces*

Joint financial endeavours and co-operative ventures generally are well accented right now. Your intuitive powers are at their peak, allowing you to weigh up any given situation almost instantly. With a slight change of emphasis, people now see you as someone who is good at talking, rather than a contentious individual.

Your Daily Guide to August 2019

19 MONDAY
Moon Age Day 19   Moon Sign Aries

If you had been planning on taking a chance in any romantic sense, now is the time to do it. Winning others round to your point of view, even beyond personal attachments, ought to be quite easy. Fortune favours the brave and you have more than a little courage on display for much of the coming week.

20 TUESDAY
Moon Age Day 20   Moon Sign Aries

You will want to deal with practical issues as quickly as you can, maybe because there are things to do that are simply for the sake of enjoyment. Don't feel guilty about this. Few people could put in more effort than you have across the last couple of weeks, so it is only fair that you also take some time to yourself.

21 WEDNESDAY
Moon Age Day 21   Moon Sign Aries

Doing things in pairs could be quite good fun now. Co-operative ventures work best for you, no matter if these are at work, or later in the day when you can get to grips with personal attachments. You won't be everyone's cup of tea today but the people who really matter are clearly on your side.

22 THURSDAY
Moon Age Day 22   Moon Sign Taurus

You need to do more of your own thing today, as opposed to pleasing others all the time. This isn't really selfish, and even if it could be considered so, you do have the right to address your own life sometimes. Avoid family disagreements, especially since you are not the one who is starting them.

23 FRIDAY
Moon Age Day 23   Moon Sign Taurus

Today could turn out to be a good deal more exciting than you might have expected. If you are at work today, look out for a chance to gain new power or responsibility. However, if you have the day to yourself, think about making changes to your social life and maybe even taking a small calculated risk.

24 SATURDAY
Moon Age Day 24   Moon Sign Gemini

Getting along with others should be very easy as the weekend gets started. It isn't usually difficult for you in any case, though there have been a few occasions in the recent past when you haven't been quite as accommodating as usual. You may have to spread tasks out in order to get them done properly.

Your Daily Guide to August 2019

25 SUNDAY
Moon Age Day 25   Moon Sign Gemini

What you hear from others can be of great use to you at present, so it is definitely worthwhile keeping your ears open today. That shouldn't be too much of an ask because Aquarius is one of the best dealers in gossip to be found anywhere within the zodiac. Look out for some small financial gains.

26 MONDAY
Moon Age Day 26   Moon Sign Cancer

There is a continued accent on work and material considerations, so much so that you might find it difficult to spend any time doing exactly what you want. When you do have free hours, you are likely to spend a good proportion of them supporting other people, particularly friends who are having difficulties.

27 TUESDAY
Moon Age Day 27   Moon Sign Cancer

This might be a period of time during which you will want to restructure elements of your life that you feel are not going the way you would wish. Instead of spending too much money today, plan how you can get more. The time for really spoiling yourself comes later, for now work hard.

28 WEDNESDAY
Moon Age Day 28   Moon Sign Leo

This is not the best time to expect to get your own way in everything. Your perspectives are somewhat obscured by the presence of the lunar low. Rather than trying to do too much in a practical or material sense, instead try spending at least a part of today doing something that pleases only you.

29 THURSDAY
Moon Age Day 29   Moon Sign Leo

If you push yourself too hard today, you are likely to run out of steam very quickly indeed. Settle for some relaxation, plus the chance to look ahead and to do some prior planning. Everyone needs to recharge their batteries once in a while and although you hardly accept the fact, Aquarius is no different.

30 FRIDAY
Moon Age Day 0   Moon Sign Virgo

What matters today is eliciting the right sort of assistance for whatever you are planning. Your astute nature and strong intuition can be brought into play and your decisions will now be quite considered. Routine tasks are undertaken easily but there is still a part of you that needs change and travel.

Your Daily Guide to August 2019

31 SATURDAY

Moon Age Day 1   Moon Sign Virgo

Pleasant encounters with others appear to be the order of the day. Your powers of attraction are now significantly increased and you have plenty of energy at your disposal. Not everyone agrees with suggestions you are making but an element of disagreement is inherent in the present astrological mix.

Your Month at a Glance

➕ = Opportunities are around ➖ = Be on the defensive ● = Life is pretty ordinary

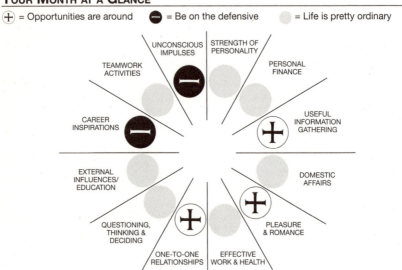

September Highs and Lows

Here I show you how the rhythms of the Moon will affect you this month. Like the tide, your energies and abilities will rise and fall with its pattern. When it is above the centre line, go for it, when it is below, you should be resting.

HIGH 10TH–12TH
LOW 25TH–26TH

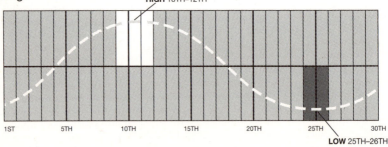

Your Daily Guide to September 2019

1 SUNDAY   *Moon Age Day 2   Moon Sign Libra*

This might be a good time to look at the way your life is structured and a period for making necessary changes. It's late in the year for a spring clean but that is more or less what seems to be happening. Don't keep hold of anything simply for the sake of habit. You may have to be slightly ruthless.

2 MONDAY   *Moon Age Day 3   Moon Sign Libra*

If you have any problems today, turn on your intuition and see what it is telling you. Understanding what makes others tick should be quite easy and you can make some real gains as a result. You are very sympathetic at present and would be quite willing to change your own direction in life a little in order to help someone else.

3 TUESDAY   *Moon Age Day 4   Moon Sign Scorpio*

You could do a lot worse today than spreading your wings. Travel hasn't been uppermost in the mind of Aquarians as much this year as is sometimes the case, though wanderlust is likely to begin to play a part in your thinking from now on. This would be an ideal time to take a holiday.

4 WEDNESDAY   *Moon Age Day 5   Moon Sign Scorpio*

Pressures can come thick and fast at work, though you might dismiss most of them with a shrug. Even when you have managed to climb a series of mountains to get what you want from life, further peaks are in view. It is possible you are trying just a little too hard and that you would benefit from a reduction in pace.

5 THURSDAY   *Moon Age Day 6   Moon Sign Scorpio*

Now you discover a period of change coming upon you. It is possible that one or two friendships have run their course. You don't want to hurt anyone, so you simply retreat from situations you now find boring. Some sort of explanation may be called for, even if you have to bend the truth slightly.

6 FRIDAY   *Moon Age Day 7   Moon Sign Sagittarius*

Emotional matters may get quite intense today so take care not to get drawn into any arguments. It might appear that people you are usually close to are singularly failing to understand or fall in line with your point of view. A little respect all round seems to be necessary.

Your *Daily Guide to September 2019*

7 SATURDAY
Moon Age Day 8   Moon Sign Sagittarius

Get out and about if you can, the further the better. You could be quieter than usual but will fare better when visiting places you haven't seen before. Likewise, you may find strangers easier to get along with than people you have known for a long time. This may also be a period for puzzles of one sort or another.

8 SUNDAY
Moon Age Day 9   Moon Sign Capricorn

Financial matters could make life feel very secure. There is more cash about than would often be the case, some of it likely to come from rather unexpected directions. Conforming to expectations could be rather difficult and you won't relish routine tasks, which you see as being very boring at present.

9 MONDAY
Moon Age Day 10   Moon Sign Capricorn

The pace of everyday events goes up a notch or two and you should find some exciting events coming along, even if you have to manufacture at least some of these yourself. Trends indicate your mind being dragged towards the past, either by events or people you haven't seen for ages.

10 TUESDAY
Moon Age Day 11   Moon Sign Aquarius

An excellent time for making fresh starts and for coming to terms with the fact that situations generally are looking up. Materially speaking, you are now likely to be doing rather better than of late. Your general level of good luck is worth putting to the test and this would be a good time for signing contracts or other documents.

11 WEDNESDAY
Moon Age Day 12   Moon Sign Aquarius

The lunar high continues, making certain you will spend at least today looking for as many good times as you can find. The joking, mischievous side of your nature is clearly on display, to the amusement of practically everyone. Be sure of yourself today and you may get more than you expected.

12 THURSDAY
Moon Age Day 13   Moon Sign Aquarius

You can attract the best of company now, though you can be in quite a grumpy frame of mind too. If there are problems, these are likely to come from the recesses of your own mind and may not be rooted in reality. In particular, avoid worrying about situations you cannot alter.

Your Daily Guide to September 2019

13 FRIDAY
Moon Age Day 14   Moon Sign Pisces

Hopeful news looks likely to be coming your way from far off places. Any Aquarian who has been looking forward to a long journey may not have to wait much longer. There are gains to be made from family members, some of whom are coming up with extremely good ideas at present.

14 SATURDAY
Moon Age Day 15   Moon Sign Pisces

Social matters could be somewhat hectic today, although you could well stumble across enjoyable situations without actually planning any of them. This would not be a good time to get involved in arguments, especially those that crop up in your family or immediate friendship circle.

15 SUNDAY
Moon Age Day 16   Moon Sign Aries

Some self-sacrifice is going to be called for today, in order to offer support to someone you care about deeply. This might mean turning away from a situation you know would be advantageous. However, being the sort of person you are, people come before any sort of pecuniary or material gain.

16 MONDAY
Moon Age Day 17   Moon Sign Aries

This would be as good a time as any to re-evaluate your finances. It could be that you have been spending rather too much of late or maybe you simply want to rein in your spending in order to save for something. When you get to work things out, it is possible you will be better off than you thought.

17 TUESDAY
Moon Age Day 18   Moon Sign Aries

Aquarius now becomes a very deep thinker but in a practical sense it might be better to do things for yourself now rather than waiting for others to get themselves moving. You have what it takes to get to the top but your attitude is slightly more considered and the actions you take more likely to pay off.

18 WEDNESDAY
Moon Age Day 19   Moon Sign Taurus

You should be finding a great deal of support coming from loved ones and from your partner especially. People may prove to be helpful in fairly unexpected ways and you are happier to lean on friends now than you sometimes are. No person is an island and that is especially true of those born under Aquarius.

Your Daily Guide to September 2019

19 THURSDAY
Moon Age Day 20   Moon Sign Taurus

You will probably find that there is more money available now than you have been expecting and that means you could tend to go over the top with spending. This would be a mistake because you might shell out too much for something that would be much cheaper in a few days. Keep your eyes open for sales.

20 FRIDAY
Moon Age Day 21   Moon Sign Gemini

In a practical sense you should be streets ahead at the moment. Whilst others struggle to get things done, you are finished with one job and well on with the next. Watch out for a little envy coming from colleagues but deal with this gently. Accept that not everyone has your ingenuity or common sense.

21 SATURDAY
Moon Age Day 22   Moon Sign Gemini

Life looks interesting enough but there may be low spots if you don't keep up the pressure yourself. What you really don't need at the moment is to become bored with your lot and that means arranging situations so that you don't have time to sit and contemplate too much. Friends should still be up for a good time.

22 SUNDAY
Moon Age Day 23   Moon Sign Gemini

The need for wide open spaces and personal freedom is as strong as ever and in fact probably even more noticeable now than generally. You want to break down fences and move into new areas of life. One step at a time is the way forward, no matter how anxious you may feel to do everything at once.

23 MONDAY
Moon Age Day 24   Moon Sign Cancer

Your opinionated views make informed communication difficult at this time. Do try to create a good social atmosphere as much as you can and don't be too aloof, no matter who you are dealing with. This probably won't be the best day of the month and you might be best spending some time on your own.

24 TUESDAY
Moon Age Day 25   Moon Sign Cancer

Everyday life is likely to feel rather complex and you may have difficulty dealing with the actions and reactions of loved ones especially. Take things in your stride as much as possible and be willing to work slowly towards personal objectives. People who really matter should come good before the end of the day.

Your Daily Guide to September 2019

25 WEDNESDAY
Moon Age Day 26   Moon Sign Leo

If there isn't a great deal in the way of assistance around today, you might feel you are going it alone. Try to remember that part of what is happening is related to your emotional state, which in turn responds to the lunar low. Slow and steady wins the race, even if this particular lap is not too eventful.

26 THURSDAY
Moon Age Day 27   Moon Sign Leo

Another day during which you cannot make the sort of headway you would wish, though you remain fairly relaxed so it might not matter all that much. Certainly you can enjoy yourself and having a good time is as important as getting on in life. Friends should prove to be quite supportive if you give them the chance.

27 FRIDAY
Moon Age Day 28   Moon Sign Virgo

An improved phase generally makes it possible for you to do some important forward planning, but you are also likely to be extremely active on the social front. Get-togethers with people you find interesting are likely to be good and you won't be at all standoffish, as could have been the case recently.

28 SATURDAY
Moon Age Day 0   Moon Sign Virgo

Money wise, the most casual of discussions could lead to important conclusions. Although you are probably not spending freely at the moment, when you do dip into your purse or wallet it is likely to be for bargains of one sort or another. Help is around when you need it, especially from relatives.

29 SUNDAY
Moon Age Day 1   Moon Sign Libra

Now there are positive highlights surrounding group activities and your present ability to expand the number of people you count as your friends. You won't go short of attention and even romance looks to be a very positive area of life. You may now rely less on a particular individual, which is a good thing.

30 MONDAY
Moon Age Day 2   Moon Sign Libra

Expect some good news today and be prepared to entertain new ideas that are put forward by family members or good friends. Although you may not be exactly dynamic in your attitude, you do have what it takes to get ahead. Social trends are far better now than those associated with business.

October 2019

Your Month at a Glance

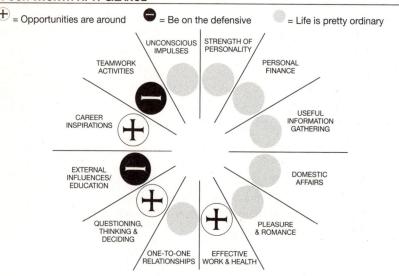

October Highs and Lows

Here I show you how the rhythms of the Moon will affect you this month. Like the tide, your energies and abilities will rise and fall with its pattern. When it is above the centre line, go for it, when it is below, you should be resting.

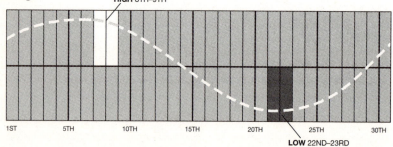

Your Daily Guide to October 2019

1 TUESDAY   *Moon Age Day 3   Moon Sign Scorpio*

You may need the bright lights of the social world to cheer you up today. There are a number of astrological reasons to explain why you are slightly down in the dumps, though there is no real reason to let these spoil your day. Keep in the mainstream at work and avoid unnecessary controversy.

2 WEDNESDAY   *Moon Age Day 4   Moon Sign Scorpio*

Some skilful manoeuvring may be necessary if you want to avoid family members falling out with each other. Although you won't necessarily make much material progress today, your ability to sort out the problems of those around you should be pleasing enough in its own right.

3 THURSDAY   *Moon Age Day 5   Moon Sign Sagittarius*

This is a good day to be on the move and to be saying what you think, especially about practical situations. The real gains today might well be romantic. New attachments should be working well under prevailing trends, whilst established ones seem to have new zest and vitality that you are bringing to them.

4 FRIDAY   *Moon Age Day 6   Moon Sign Sagittarius*

The best advice that can be offered to Aquarius today is to ensure that you get one task out of the way before you start on another. There is a danger of overlap and confusion that you could so easily avoid. There ought to be a good deal of happiness about in a family and friendship sense.

5 SATURDAY   *Moon Age Day 7   Moon Sign Capricorn*

Improved communication is likely to be the best gift of the weekend. Don't be tardy when it comes to expressing an opinion, even when you know there are people around who will not agree with you. Although you won't be feeling absolutely positive about everything, you can fool others and even yourself in the end.

6 SUNDAY   *Moon Age Day 8   Moon Sign Capricorn*

All joint financial matters are especially well-starred at present, likewise partnerships with a monetary aspect. In addition, you should find it easier to whisper those intimate little words that can make all the difference in the relationship stakes. Don't be too quick to jump to conclusions in the workplace.

Your Daily Guide to October 2019

7 MONDAY
Moon Age Day 9   Moon Sign Capricorn

There are certain signposts to success around now, even if you have to keep your eyes wide open in order to recognise them. Socially speaking, you are anxious to meet new people and may well give some of your associations from the past the order of the boot! Aquarius is all about change and diversity at present.

8 TUESDAY
Moon Age Day 10   Moon Sign Aquarius

Planetary benefits come along from a number of different directions whilst the lunar high is present. You can afford to back your hunches and might find yourself sought out by someone you think of as being extremely special. Although the summer has now definitely ended you may decide to spend time out of doors.

9 WEDNESDAY
Moon Age Day 11   Moon Sign Aquarius

Plans should be turning out more or less as you would expect, leaving you with hours on your hands that can simply be used to have fun. There are some particularly interesting people around, one or two of whom have had their eye on you for a while. Affection comes from some very surprising directions.

10 THURSDAY
Moon Age Day 12   Moon Sign Pisces

Although you should be in a good frame of mind today, it is by no means certain that the people you work with are in a wonderful mood. Clearly, some patience is necessary. Aquarius is lucky in this respect because it has plenty of Air-sign get-up-and-go but it is a natural peacemaker and negotiator.

11 FRIDAY
Moon Age Day 13   Moon Sign Pisces

You will now enjoy keeping a high profile, whether at work or out there in the social world. You can probably expect good news somewhere in the family, perhaps associated with a new arrival. Concern for your partner may be quite understandable but is probably without real foundation.

12 SATURDAY
Moon Age Day 14   Moon Sign Pisces

Although you may not be at work today, the very best astrological trends appear to be pointing in that direction. For this reason, Aquarians who work on a Saturday score highest on the planetary scale today. At home, you may find some of the things that are happening to be tedious and maybe even pointless.

Your Daily Guide to October 2019

13 SUNDAY
Moon Age Day 15   Moon Sign Aries

Travel is definitely recommended both now and in the week ahead. In sporting activities, you could be doing rather better than you had expected, partly because you are so very competitive right now. A warm and wonderful sort of evening is yours for the taking, if you line up the right person.

14 MONDAY
Moon Age Day 16   Moon Sign Aries

The potential for getting what you want across the board sense is strong today. There are people around who actively want to offer you help and support and you should be able to locate them easily enough. Conforming to the expectations that older relatives have of you could be somewhat complicated.

15 TUESDAY
Moon Age Day 17   Moon Sign Taurus

Your desire to please others might fall flat but that is no reason to avoid trying. The area of life that works best for you appears to be that of romance. Finding the right words to say 'I love you' should be quite easy now and the response you get will make the effort more than worthwhile.

16 WEDNESDAY
Moon Age Day 18   Moon Sign Taurus

Input from others into your personal ambitions is noteworthy and this would be a good day for a family chat. Those you care about the most are showing their affection for you and even though you might not make a lot of material progress today it really doesn't matter too much. Aquarius needs to feel secure and should do so now.

17 THURSDAY
Moon Age Day 19   Moon Sign Taurus

You may encounter some unconventional or unusual sorts of people today. Today offers a good deal in personal terms but you might have a little difficulty getting on-side with younger family members. In the main, the best trends come from personal attachments and friendships.

18 FRIDAY
Moon Age Day 20   Moon Sign Gemini

This is one of the best days of the month on which to broaden your horizons in any way possible. Journeys, both long and short, tend to be very enjoyable and you can gain a great deal from being out there in the world doing whatever takes your fancy. The only problems come if you feel in any way restricted.

Your Daily Guide to October 2019

19 SATURDAY
Moon Age Day 21   Moon Sign Gemini

Be more adventurous and, if possible, give in to the need within you to seek out new horizons. The desire for stimulating new situations is extremely strong and the gains you can make on the way are many. Aquarius doesn't generally like to be tied down too much and this is certainly the case now.

20 SUNDAY
Moon Age Day 22   Moon Sign Cancer

Some of the experiences you have with regard to love are likely to be more intense now. Some of your basic attitudes to life have to be reappraised and there is also a need to listen very carefully to what your partner is saying. There can be confusion about today but also a good deal of happiness.

21 MONDAY
Moon Age Day 23   Moon Sign Cancer

New assistance could easily be on offer where your professional life is concerned and it would be somewhat foolish to turn away from this just because you want to plough your own furrow. People genuinely want to help and will be very pleased if you accept their offers.

22 TUESDAY
Moon Age Day 24   Moon Sign Leo

If anything, you are being slightly less consistent today, a good indication that you are not working at your best. Perhaps you need to look at certain matters with more care and it would help to keep quiet about them until you have. There are gains to be made, though you will have to look hard to find them.

23 WEDNESDAY
Moon Age Day 25   Moon Sign Leo

Continuing yesterday's trends, you are quiet and contemplative today. Although you won't personally see this as a problem, people who have great expectations of you might. It should not be difficult to explain yourself and, in any case, by tomorrow afternoon the Moon will have moved out of Leo. Delaying tactics are called for.

24 THURSDAY
Moon Age Day 26   Moon Sign Virgo

Today's highlights tend to come as a result of stimulating discussions on a variety of subjects. There's nothing strange about this as far as Aquarius is concerned but it is a fact that you are even more enthusiastic about life than usual. Whether or not the sun shines today, there is plenty of warmth emanating from you.

Your Daily Guide to October 2019

25 FRIDAY
Moon Age Day 27   Moon Sign Virgo

This would be a very good day for any sort of trip undertaken more or less solely for the sake of pleasure. If you plan a shopping spree there is a good chance you will be in for a bargain. Meanwhile, learning and intellectual interests of all kinds really stimulate you to make significant personal progress.

26 SATURDAY
Moon Age Day 28   Moon Sign Libra

Now you should concentrate more on reliable long-term plans for a while. Some of these look like they will begin to start bearing fruit and you wouldn't want to let go of incentives that have been a long time in the making. Saturday could offer you the time to think about things much more positively.

27 SUNDAY
Moon Age Day 0   Moon Sign Libra

Much energy is now channelled into professional ambitions but you must make sure to avoid arrogance, even when you know what you are talking about and you are certain that others do not. Confidence does not give you the right to lord it over others. Aquarius can sometimes be too single-minded for its own good.

28 MONDAY
Moon Age Day 1   Moon Sign Scorpio

You may now benefit from keeping up a fairly high profile, though it is one in which you play a friendly and approachable part. Putting on the right mental costume for whatever life throws at you is second nature to an Aquarian and you will certainly be doing so effectively under present astrological trends.

29 TUESDAY
Moon Age Day 2   Moon Sign Scorpio

Your gut instincts are definitely worth following as the new week continues. A little luck is on your side and you are in the mood to take a few chances. A feeling that almost anything is possible turns out to be correct and there are few obstacles to block your path. In social situations and romance you are presently charming.

30 WEDNESDAY
Moon Age Day 3   Moon Sign Sagittarius

Good organisation and preparation seems to be the major key to success as far as business initiatives are concerned. Competition might be somewhat tough but that won't bother you because you know what you are doing and how to get round difficulties. Friends and relatives should be very supportive.

31 THURSDAY   *Moon Age Day 4   Moon Sign Sagittarius*

You might be surprised to discover just how much others are willing to give way to your point of view at present. This is not a time for arguments but for genuine discussions to open up your personal point of view. People find you stimulating to have around and the very unusual view of life you often adopt is refreshing to them.

November 2019

Your Month at a Glance

⊕ = Opportunities are around ⊖ = Be on the defensive ○ = Life is pretty ordinary

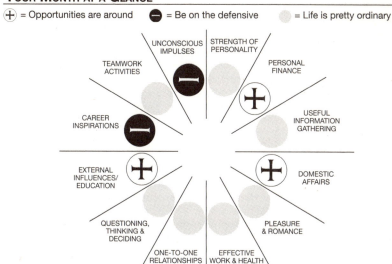

November Highs and Lows

Here I show you how the rhythms of the Moon will affect you this month. Like the tide, your energies and abilities will rise and fall with its pattern. When it is above the centre line, go for it, when it is below, you should be resting.

HIGH 4TH–5TH

LOW 18TH–20TH

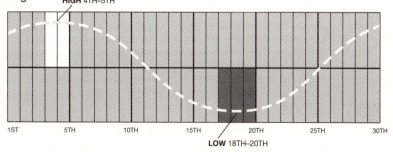

Your Daily Guide to November 2019

1 FRIDAY ☿   *Moon Age Day 5   Moon Sign Sagittarius*

The emphasis today is on life's more playful aspects. It might be hard to take anything too seriously, at least until after the weekend. However, your offbeat sense of humour and off-the-wall attitude will be popular with almost everyone and can actually lead to you achieving a great deal.

2 SATURDAY ☿   *Moon Age Day 6   Moon Sign Capricorn*

Be careful when it comes to listening to gossip. There is a good chance that much of what you hear today is either misleading or downright wrong. Opt for some fresh air if you can. This is Saturday after all and locking yourself into the house won't be good for you, mentally or physically.

3 SUNDAY ☿   *Moon Age Day 7   Moon Sign Capricorn*

This is a particularly good time to pursue intellectual interests or philosophical investigations. All Aquarians want to know what makes the world the way it is and speculation is very healthy for you. Of course, you won't get to all the answers but you can have fun trying.

4 MONDAY ☿   *Moon Age Day 8   Moon Sign Aquarius*

The lunar high should find you fighting fit and anxious to make the best sort of impression. If there is any fly in the ointment at all, it could be that not everyone you come across is equally helpful. Put your best foot forward at work but leave time for personal enjoyment coming your way later in the day.

5 TUESDAY ☿   *Moon Age Day 9   Moon Sign Aquarius*

The go-ahead influence continues and you find people rather more willing to listen to your suggestions now. Part of the reason for this is your persuasive tongue and you won't have much trouble bringing people round to your point of view. Romance is especially well-starred for those on the lookout for it.

6 WEDNESDAY ☿   *Moon Age Day 10   Moon Sign Pisces*

Though some obstacles may get in the way at work, socially and romantically, you appear to be on top form. Consideration for family members and friends comes as second nature to you, though you won't always be able to help them quite to the extent you might wish. The generally progressive phase continues.

Your Daily Guide to November 2019

7 THURSDAY ☿ Moon Age Day 11   Moon Sign Pisces

You could be rather socially reluctant today, which might not appear to bode well for the day as a whole. This probably isn't the case. You are likely to be very good when mixing with people you know well and only demonstrate a degree of reserve when having to deal with those who are virtual strangers.

8 FRIDAY ☿ Moon Age Day 12   Moon Sign Pisces

You don't lack confidence, even though your actions are somewhat subdued. You won't have long to wait for things to get moving again and in the meantime, you can enjoy watching life go by, and not worry about being at the front of every queue. Concern for family members could be great but is probably not justified.

9 SATURDAY ☿ Moon Age Day 13   Moon Sign Aries

Your attention may be called to specific hitches that come along this Saturday. Perhaps arrangements you have made don't come off or you could have to reorganise things at the last minute. Family members might not be especially helpful at a time when you could do with some positive input.

10 SUNDAY ☿ Moon Age Day 14   Moon Sign Aries

Your charming and playful side is now clearly on display. Don't be too distracted by the fun and games that are available because there is plenty for you to do in practical sense. Many Aquarians are now looking at the possibility of making changes to their living environments.

11 MONDAY ☿ Moon Age Day 15   Moon Sign Taurus

It looks as though professional matters are well-starred at the moment, even if it doesn't seem to be that way at first. When you are faced with awkward people today, turn on that natural charm and watch situations change quickly. You might need a good deal of give and take in your relationship.

12 TUESDAY ☿ Moon Age Day 16   Moon Sign Taurus

It appears that you are on the lookout for new acquaintances. If this means you have become somewhat bored with your usual social crowd, think about a new interest or pastime that you would find stimulating. You need to keep those grey cells working and cannot stand feeling bored.

Your Daily Guide to November 2019

13 WEDNESDAY ☿
Moon Age Day 17   Moon Sign Taurus

If you find yourself under any pressure today, it is likely to come from the direction of people who could be a little jealous of you. Take this situation in your stride because this is definitely not a day to give as good as you get. By remaining composed, you will win the battle in the end.

14 THURSDAY ☿
Moon Age Day 18   Moon Sign Gemini

The focus now shifts to the social arena. If there are any invitations on offer today, grab them with both hands. You need the support of friends and relatives if you are going to get the very best out of any given situation. What you don't need is to be nagged, so stay away from people who insist on moaning about anything.

15 FRIDAY ☿
Moon Age Day 19   Moon Sign Gemini

The domestic scene looks to be your main area of success at the moment. It isn't that you fail to make a positive impression in a professional way, merely that most of your interest is associated in some way with hearth and home. Maybe you are planning some alterations or are already busy with DIY.

16 SATURDAY ☿
Moon Age Day 20   Moon Sign Cancer

At the start of the weekend it might seem that you work much better in groups. Aquarius is a social animal at the best of times but much more so now. The only difficulty today would be if circumstances forced you to spend long periods of time relying on your own company.

17 SUNDAY ☿
Moon Age Day 21   Moon Sign Cancer

Get on with practical matters today. Although your workload could be on the increase, this should not prove to be too much of a problem. Not only are you very capable at the moment but you will also discover that there is significant assistance around if you want to call on it.

18 MONDAY ☿
Moon Age Day 22   Moon Sign Leo

There is a temporary lull beginning today. You don't want it and will fight against it but facts are facts. What you can do very well at the moment is to think. Looking ahead, making plans and getting yourself into a more favourable position generally is going to be both important and relevant.

Your Daily Guide to November 2019

19 TUESDAY ☿   *Moon Age Day 23   Moon Sign Leo*

The fewer mistakes you make today, the better you are going to feel about life as a whole. Concentration might not be easy but you will win through if you simply employ a degree of dogged determination. Don't necessarily expect a high degree of co-operation, even from people who usually lend a hand.

20 WEDNESDAY ☿   *Moon Age Day 24   Moon Sign Leo*

People in positions of authority are now more approachable. The planets say this would be a good time for signing documents and for making financial decisions about the longer-term future. You might have to come to terms with a truth that is not all that palatable but which is necessary.

21 THURSDAY   *Moon Age Day 25   Moon Sign Virgo*

Right now the time is favourable for job changes or a move upwards. The planets at the moment are good for all enterprises involving co-operation with others and compromises are especially important if you want to make the best possible use of what surrounds you. Romantically speaking you should be on fine form.

22 FRIDAY   *Moon Age Day 26   Moon Sign Virgo*

Work taking place in a team should be running nicely for you at present. For this you can thank the Sun, which enters your solar eleventh house around now. Another consequence is that your perceived popularity is on the increase. Make use of this by asking for one or two things you really want.

23 SATURDAY   *Moon Age Day 27   Moon Sign Libra*

Minor changes to your thinking can make goals and objectives more certain so there is a great need for flexibility at this time. Don't be held back by the negative attitude of one or two people. Even though they may seem to have had influence in the past, these people have little or nothing to do with your life as it stands.

24 SUNDAY   *Moon Age Day 28   Moon Sign Libra*

You seem to be pretty much in demand in a social sense and won't really have all much time to do what pleases only you. Giving yourself to others and to situations generally can be quite exhausting under current trends, but you have what it takes to make the world laugh, and that's a great gift.

Your Daily Guide to November 2019

25 MONDAY
Moon Age Day 29   Moon Sign Scorpio

Others at work, or in professional circles generally, might appear somewhat pushy and difficult to deal with. Treat this situation with as much optimism and humour as you can and don't be pushed into falling out with anyone. Your general attitude to life is good and you can make a joke even out of adversity.

26 TUESDAY
Moon Age Day 0   Moon Sign Scorpio

Many of the little problems you encounter at the moment are likely to be resolved thanks to a very deep intuition on your part. You won't have to work hard to see how any particular situation is likely to work out and you don't need your practical skills right now half as much as your instincts.

27 WEDNESDAY
Moon Age Day 1   Moon Sign Sagittarius

Life ought to be fairly sweet today, especially on the social front. There is suddenly less of a professional incentive and you really just want to enjoy yourself. Getting together with friends would prove to be good and you are also casting an eye forward to a Christmas that is not all that far ahead.

28 THURSDAY
Moon Age Day 2   Moon Sign Sagittarius

Don't take situations or people for granted today. It's important to know what others are thinking and to react accordingly. This might not be easy because there is a noticeable lazy streak surrounding you at present. Make sure that you do at least one surprising thing today and don't turn away from anything exciting.

29 FRIDAY
Moon Age Day 3   Moon Sign Capricorn

Friendships hit a definite high note around now and you remain essentially a social animal. You can't be on the ball all the time, especially at work, and much of today will find you relaxing. Someone you haven't seen much of late is probably going to get in touch before very long.

30 SATURDAY
Moon Age Day 4   Moon Sign Capricorn

Make the most of familiar people and places this weekend. There isn't really the incentive about to push for change or diversity and you settle happily into routines of one sort or another. Aquarius should be very content with its lot under present trends, though you are far from progressive.

2019

YOUR MONTH AT A GLANCE

⊕ = Opportunities are around   ⊖ = Be on the defensive   ○ = Life is pretty ordinary

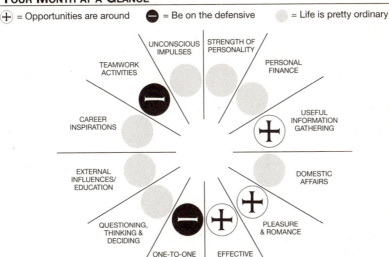

DECEMBER HIGHS AND LOWS

Here I show you how the rhythms of the Moon will affect you this month. Like the tide, your energies and abilities will rise and fall with its pattern. When it is above the centre line, go for it, when it is below, you should be resting.   **HIGH** 1ST–3RD   **HIGH** 29TH–30TH

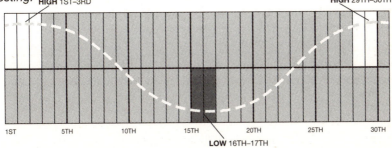

LOW 16TH–17TH

Your Daily Guide to December 2019

1 SUNDAY
Moon Age Day 5   Moon Sign Aquarius

You are persuasive and very active now. Take advantage of the positive trends by being where things are happening. This is certainly no time to hide your light under a bushel and there should be every opportunity to prove what you are capable of. Confidence grows by the minute.

2 MONDAY
Moon Age Day 6   Moon Sign Aquarius

There ought to be many more than one situation that looks good for you at this time. It is one of the jobs of Aquarius to establish a sensible balance in life, so part of you doesn't want to go over the top but it would be hard not to recognise how positive you are likely to be feeling and how good the world appears.

3 TUESDAY
Moon Age Day 7   Moon Sign Aquarius

The good things in life tend to come to you around now. This is a short-term trend brought about by the Moon but you should take advantage of it. People are likely to be very helpful and should be doing just about anything they can to assist you. Don't be too proud to accept some sound advice from a trusted friend.

4 WEDNESDAY
Moon Age Day 8   Moon Sign Pisces

There may be aspects to your home life that are proving to be somewhat tiresome. If this turns out to be the case, make alterations by spending time with your friends. If loved ones don't see quite so much of you around now they might begin to value you all the more when you are at home.

5 THURSDAY
Moon Age Day 9   Moon Sign Pisces

If there were a battle of wills taking place at home, you would be well advised to stay as clear of it as you can. Someone you don't see very often could be making a return visit to your life and they could bring an interesting offer with them. You are also likely to be contacting someone who lives far away.

6 FRIDAY
Moon Age Day 10   Moon Sign Aries

It now occurs to you that Christmas is just around the corner. Do what you have to in order to convince family members you are pulling your weight, though it's likely you won't have quite as much enthusiasm about the festive season as many people you meet. Don't worry because this state of affairs will change.

Your Daily Guide to December 2019

7 SATURDAY *Moon Age Day 11   Moon Sign Aries*

Your love life could be something of a challenge this weekend but there is nothing to indicate that anything much is going wrong for you. It could be slightly harder than usual to persuade your partner that your point of view is the right one and a good deal of coaxing may be necessary. Create a comfortable home environment now.

8 SUNDAY *Moon Age Day 12   Moon Sign Aries*

Though you are ready for action in most respects, you will have some difficulty getting other people around you moving. Acting on impulse might seem to be the best way forward and in the majority of situations it will work well enough. Avoid unnecessary rows at home by making yourself absent if necessary.

9 MONDAY *Moon Age Day 13   Moon Sign Taurus*

Perhaps there is time for a little solitude today, though maybe not. At least do your best to get short breaks during which you can simply sit and think. Although in a social sense you are fully committed to the festivities that lie ahead, part of you is not that happy with all the upheaval they create.

10 TUESDAY *Moon Age Day 14   Moon Sign Taurus*

A more relaxed social period is in view and you won't be short of attention from someone special. Your eyes may be fully on Christmas, especially if you know you haven't yet done everything to prepare yourself. At work you should be jogging along nicely but may not be exactly ecstatic at your progress all the same.

11 WEDNESDAY *Moon Age Day 15   Moon Sign Gemini*

It is likely that others find it difficult to keep up with the pace of your quick and ready mind. This means having to travel like a convoy – at the speed of the slowest ship. Whilst this may be quite frustrating in some ways, your kind nature is unlikely to allow you to behave in any other way.

12 THURSDAY *Moon Age Day 16   Moon Sign Gemini*

Creative change comes along now and is particularly noticeable in personal relationships. You may be looking at your partner in a new light, or it is possible that their very actions are causing your change of attitude. Friends are also somehow warmer than they were last week, though the real alteration is in you.

Your Daily Guide to December 2019

13 FRIDAY
Moon Age Day 17   Moon Sign Cancer

Freedom now seems to be the main key to happiness. Seek out wide-open spaces and don't restrict yourself in any way. With everything to play for in both a social and business sense, this could turn out to be one of the more fortunate days of December. Keep an eye on the plans others are making for the festive season.

14 SATURDAY
Moon Age Day 18   Moon Sign Cancer

You have now entered a period that is especially good for personal growth. There could be opportunities to broaden your horizons in a number of different ways and you also have a greater desire for excitement. Doing exactly what you wish might be difficult but you have it within you to compromise.

15 SUNDAY
Moon Age Day 19   Moon Sign Cancer

Friendships are now significant to you, and continue to be so well into the Christmas period. The present planetary array makes you softer and more yielding. It also brings a fairly nostalgic frame of mind but there is probably nothing too surprising about that during this time of the year.

16 MONDAY
Moon Age Day 20   Moon Sign Leo

Find the time to recharge your batteries today and tomorrow. Although there is still plenty to be done ahead of the festivities, you won't help yourself or anyone else if you are exhausted. There should be time today to do something that pleases just you and it ought to be something reasonably quiet.

17 TUESDAY
Moon Age Day 21   Moon Sign Leo

Another less than hectic day would probably suit you fine, though it's unlikely you will be able to please yourself two days running. Don't become involved in jobs you know are going to prove either tedious or demanding. Also keep major decisions to a minimum until at least tomorrow.

18 WEDNESDAY
Moon Age Day 22   Moon Sign Virgo

Today should prove to be a key day where general progress is concerned, even if doing exactly what you would wish so close to Christmas might not be all that easy. Part of you is committed to change but there is also a tendency to be over-nostalgic about past events. The progressive side will win out.

Your Daily Guide to December 2019

19 THURSDAY
Moon Age Day 23   Moon Sign Virgo

Great things happen in groups – and that's the way Aquarius likes it. You are rarely a solo-operator and find it easy to adapt your own character to suit that of those with whom you must interact. Co-operation is certainly the key word today and there isn't any doubting your sincerity or pleasant disposition.

20 FRIDAY
Moon Age Day 24   Moon Sign Libra

Whilst personal relationships gain from information that comes your way now, you should also find the day useful from a financial point of view. Socially speaking, things are on the up and there are some strong planetary influences coming into view that offer a greater sense of general security.

21 SATURDAY
Moon Age Day 25   Moon Sign Libra

Though you tend to go after what you want in life in a fairly urgent sort of way, you can actually get more if you take your time. You seem to be very driven at the moment and will be quite keen to make progress, even in areas where it isn't that likely. A practical matter definitely requires a more patient approach.

22 SUNDAY
Moon Age Day 26   Moon Sign Scorpio

Your social life is likely to be running more or less the way you would wish. There is much to be done at the moment and with some strong, supporting planetary influences you are efficient and generally successful. Not everyone likes your ideas but you have to realise that you can't influence the whole world.

23 MONDAY
Moon Age Day 27   Moon Sign Scorpio

There is likely to be a strong involvement now with people who have a tremendous part to play in your life, both at the moment and for the longer-term future. Whether you realise this fact or not remains to be seen but there is little doubt that someone is trying to manipulate you. You need to pay attention.

24 TUESDAY
Moon Age Day 28   Moon Sign Sagittarius

Christmas Eve for most Aquarians should be an excellent a day, and one that could bring you closer to your heart's desire than you have been for quite a while. This is likely to be an active run-up to Christmas Day but don't worry because your energy looks certain to hold out.

Your Daily Guide to December 2019

25 WEDNESDAY
Moon Age Day 29   Moon Sign Sagittarius

All in all, you should have a good Christmas Day but if you want to make it the best, it will be necessary to change a few of your ideas and go along with the crowd. Some of the surprises of the day should delight you. You might, however, need reminding that you can be slightly oversensitive about specific matters.

26 THURSDAY
Moon Age Day 0   Moon Sign Capricorn

Boxing Day, though not without its setbacks, should run smoothly enough and this in turn offers you the chance to find fun things to do. Short-term objectives should seem to be nicely on target and it is plain that you relish the social attention that is likely to come your way at present.

27 FRIDAY
Moon Age Day 1   Moon Sign Capricorn

Getting along with certain other people might not be the easiest thing in the world today, especially if you seem to have been in their company for days and days. Allow a little fresh air to blow into your life. Get out and about and seek the company of friends. You should soon feel less constrained.

28 SATURDAY
Moon Age Day 2   Moon Sign Capricorn

Enjoy your home and don't be afraid to get involved in family discussions. Needing to belong is part of what being an Aquarian is about and you are the life and soul of domestic parties. Friends prove to be very supportive too and there is a strong need to split your time between different gatherings.

29 SUNDAY
Moon Age Day 3   Moon Sign Aquarius

Your personal effectiveness is at its best today – maybe a good deal stronger than you had expected. Finishing little tasks should be easy enough and there is great excitement about, most of it created by you! Make today your own and at the same time you will bring much happiness to others.

30 MONDAY
Moon Age Day 4   Moon Sign Aquarius

You have a good ability to both think and communicate clearly. With great insight, you might even be going through a period during which you feel 'tuned in' to the world around you. Once again you demonstrate the deeper and more caring qualities of your sign and make the day good for everyone.

Your Daily Guide to December 2019

31 TUESDAY *Moon Age Day 5   Moon Sign Pisces*

You are making most of the running yourself on this New Year's Eve, and will be in the right frame of mind to party until dawn. You will relish the odd boost to your ego that comes your way. Keep things light and enjoyable and you will make the last day of the year very entertaining.

How to Calculate Your Rising Sign

Most astrologers agree that, next to the Sun Sign, the most important influence on any person is the Rising Sign at the time of their birth. The Rising Sign represents the astrological sign that was rising over the eastern horizon when each and every one of us came into the world. It is sometimes also called the Ascendant.

Let us suppose, for example, that you were born with the Sun in the zodiac sign of Libra. This would bestow certain characteristics on you that are likely to be shared by all other Librans. However, a Libran with Aries Rising would show a very different attitude towards life, and of course relationships, than a Libran with Pisces Rising.

For these reasons, this book shows how your zodiac Rising Sign has a bearing on all the possible positions of the Sun at birth. Simply look through the Aries table opposite.

As long as you know your approximate time of birth the graph will show you how to discover your Rising Sign.

Look across the top of the graph of your zodiac sign to find your date of birth, and down the side for your birth time (I have used Greenwich Mean Time). Where they cross is your Rising Sign. Don't forget to subtract an hour (or two) if appropriate for Summer Time.

Rising Signs for Aquarius

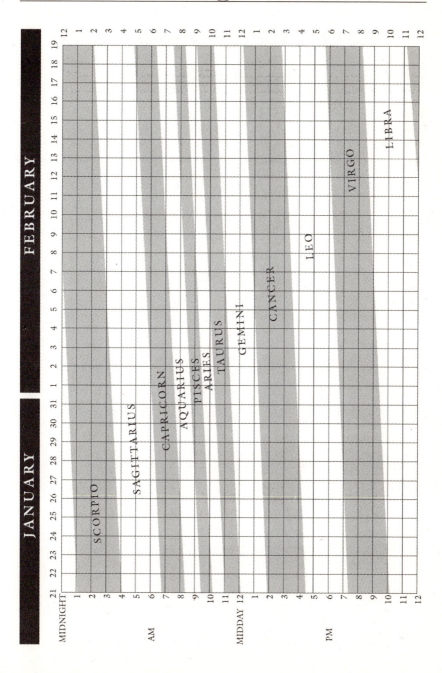

THE ZODIAC, PLANETS AND CORRESPONDENCES

The Earth revolves around the Sun once every calendar year, so when viewed from Earth the Sun appears in a different part of the sky as the year progresses. In astrology, these parts of the sky are divided into the signs of the zodiac and this means that the signs are organised in a circle. The circle begins with Aries and ends with Pisces.

Taking the zodiac sign as a starting point, astrologers then work with all the positions of planets, stars and many other factors to calculate horoscopes and birth charts and tell us what the stars have in store for us.

The table below shows the planets and Elements for each of the signs of the zodiac. Each sign belongs to one of the four Elements: Fire, Air, Earth or Water. Fire signs are creative and enthusiastic; Air signs are mentally active and thoughtful; Earth signs are constructive and practical; Water signs are emotional and have strong feelings.

It also shows the metals and gemstones associated with, or corresponding with, each sign. The correspondence is made when a metal or stone possesses properties that are held in common with a particular sign of the zodiac.

Finally, the table shows the opposite of each star sign – this is the opposite sign in the astrological circle.

Placed	Sign	Symbol	Element	Planet	Metal	Stone	Opposite
1	Aries	Ram	Fire	Mars	Iron	Bloodstone	Libra
2	Taurus	Bull	Earth	Venus	Copper	Sapphire	Scorpio
3	Gemini	Twins	Air	Mercury	Mercury	Tiger's Eye	Sagittarius
4	Cancer	Crab	Water	Moon	Silver	Pearl	Capricorn
5	Leo	Lion	Fire	Sun	Gold	Ruby	Aquarius
6	Virgo	Maiden	Earth	Mercury	Mercury	Sardonyx	Pisces
7	Libra	Scales	Air	Venus	Copper	Sapphire	Aries
8	Scorpio	Scorpion	Water	Pluto	Plutonium	Jasper	Taurus
9	Sagittarius	Archer	Fire	Jupiter	Tin	Topaz	Gemini
10	Capricorn	Goat	Earth	Saturn	Lead	Black Onyx	Cancer
11	Aquarius	Waterbearer	Air	Uranus	Uranium	Amethyst	Leo
12	Pisces	Fishes	Water	Neptune	Tin	Moonstone	Virgo